TEARING AT THE SEAMS

TRIBALISM
IN
POSTMODERN
AMERICA

ERIC
ROBERT
MORSE

NEW
CLASSIC
BOOKS

Tearing at the Seams

Essays first published in various periodicals 2015-20. This collection published in 2021 by

New Classic Books. All rights reserved. Printed in the United States of America. No part of

this book may be used or reproduced in any manner whatsoever without written permission

except in the case of brief quotations embodied in critical articles and reviews.

For information, contact:

Code Publishing

www.code-interactive.com

ISBN 1-60020-066-4

978-1-60020-066-3

CONTENTS

AUTHOR'S NOTE

In a 2020 Election Day interview, *New York Times* columnist David Brooks lamented that he had to spend the last four years writing about politics. He would much rather have spent the time discussing culture or emotions, but, since Trump entered the White House, politics was the only thing people seemed to care about. So he begrudgingly wrote about it.

The assumption was that Trump brought with him a complete upheaval of socio-political norms and introduced a threat to democracy that America had not seen up to that time. If he could be ousted, all of that would change. There wouldn't be such a polarizing figure at the helm, and so everyone could get back to living normal lives.

And this is exactly how mainstream media reacted after the election. When Biden was announced winner it was as if all of the problems America had faced had been happily wiped away. The convulsion had been caused by Orange Man Bad, and, now that he was gone, there would be unity and peace again.

Of course, the lunacy that has followed the election should indicate otherwise. Roving bands of visigoths sacking the Capitol, SJW witch hunts more merciless than ever. What discord there was in the Trump years is only getting worse.

What if all the turmoil of the last four years wasn't caused by Trump after all? What if something else is going on?

The fact is, the problems we're facing are much deeper and pervasive than a single man, no matter his hue of umber. Trump was not the cause of our ills; he was a symptom. And you don't cure a headache by chopping off your head. If we want to get back to living normal lives as Brooks would have it, it will take more than just hating Trump into oblivion.

Orwell wrote, "In our age there is no such thing as 'keeping out of politics.' All issues are political issues, and politics itself is a mass of lies, evasions, folly, hatred and schizophrenia." It is a lovely thought that getting rid of Trump will put an end to the rift. But the open-eyed observer will realize that, if we don't address the root of the divisiveness, the conflict will only worsen and we will never get back to leading normal lives.

So, what is at the root of the divisiveness? Cultural historian Jacques Barzun explained that "An age is unified by one or two pressing needs, not by the proposed remedies, which are many and thus divide." What is most fascinating about our hyper-social age is that the pressing needs that unite us are also the forces that separate us: interdependence, diversity, individuality, equality, identity. We are unified by what divides us; we are united by divisiveness.

The result is something of a social Chinese handcuff—the more we pull ourselves apart, the more confined we become. A CBS News poll recently found that, according to Americans, the biggest threat to America's way of life is "Other people in America". Everywhere we find what Dostoyevsky called 'Nadryvy'—'Ruptures', 'Strains', 'Torments', 'Crises', 'Crack-Ups', 'Lacerations'. Yeats' poesy never rang truer: "Things fall apart; the centre cannot hold".

As such, we find ourselves on the brink—of separation, of secession, of civil war. The States are no longer United. The National Anthem that we used to sing at baseball games and graduation ceremonies before COVID lockdowns outlawed community is aptly framed as a question: Despite our travails, does the flag still fly? In 1812, it was a practical question as to whether the fledgling U.S. troops had stood their ground against the overnight siege by the British. These days, in our collective dark night of the soul, the question is reversed. The flag is still here, but does it still fly over such a thing as the land of the free and home of the brave?

It is the same question that Hamilton posed in Federalist 1: "Whether societies of men are really capable or not, of establishing good government from reflection and choice, or whether they are forever destined to depend, for their political constitutions, on accident and force."

The following essays are an attempt to explore the implications of this question, by turns examining the philosophical error at the heart of our ills, the cultural decay that stems from it, the divide that it causes, and the conflict that ultimately results. Charles Kettering said "A problem well-stated is half-solved." Though these essays do not wholly solve the problem, it is the belief of the author that they state it well, and thereby lead us in the direction of a lasting solution.

—E.R.M.

Boerne, TX, January 2021

THE
WOKE

THE GREAT AWOKENING

Show a picture of 2020 to the average American of 1999 and he'd be incredulous. Surely, he'd think, there is more to the future than Antifa-chic 'influencers' snapping selfies with their surgical masks and BLM signs in front of burned-out police stations. No flying cars or hoverboards. Just doctorate-level offense archeology and weaponized unfriending.

You'd have to convince our unbelieving time traveler that we spent the entire year locked in basements for fear of a virus that had a 99.7% survival rate. It wouldn't help to explain that we were just 'following the science', which in the year 2020 meant blindly obeying the latest diktat handed down by power-tripping Orwellian demagogues. Twenty years ago, the term 'science' maintained at least a semblance of its original meaning and scientists were expected to question and analyze. Today, 'science' means 'Do as you are told by people who are better than you'. We hear the phrase 'The science is settled' and all debate is put to rest, despite the fact that anyone with a modicum of understanding knows that the nature of science is to never be settled.

Of course, we were allowed to escape the confines of our cellars in order to shop for the necessities such as canned goods and toilet paper, but only at Big-Brother-approved big-box mega stores like Walmart and Target, which were magically exempt from the plague, or in order to protest other public health risks like systemic racism or white supremacy, which the science-is-settled crowd had determined to be deadlier than the virus ever was. In 2020, science told us that you could kill grandma if you gathered in large crowds, unless the assembly was intended to fight racism or to celebrate the defeat of Donald Trump, in which case it was compulsory.

There were a few in 2020 who didn't realize that 'science' had been redefined as 'conformity' and kept challenging what they saw as inconsistent and unreasonable lock-down measures. This kept the science-is-settled crowd Karening everywhere they went until Jack Dorsey and Mark Zuckerberg finally agreed to do the most science-is-settled-y thing possible and censor content that opposed the grand unified settledness. At first, they tried to filter dissident content with party-line propaganda-pushers unironically called 'fact-checkers'. When they caught themselves fact-checking op-eds and satire, they just started deleting everything that they didn't like.

And there was plenty for them not to like. Many Americans in 2020 still believed that men are men and women are women and that saying that you're a unicorn doesn't make it so. The science-is-settled gestapo had their hands full trying to persuade these Stone Age troglodytes that gender is a social construct but that you need state-funded hormone therapy and surgeries to be transgender and that some men have uteruses and that anyone can be a woman but that masculinity is toxic so we should make women more like men. This year, 'Baby It's Cold Outside' was degrading, but 'WAP' was empowering. Apparently, the devil announced that his preferred pronouns are 'Legion'.

In 2020, the science had been settled that words are violence, riots are peaceful, and 2+2=5. Anyone caught questioning it was to be hunted down and Tweeted alive. In 2020, 2+2=5ers were like the witch hunters of 1620 but with multicolored flags.

Our time-traveler friend would be particularly intrigued by the resurgence of racial tensions in America, which had all but disappeared by the end of the 1990s. We'd have to inform him that, like 'science', the word 'racism' no longer meant what he thought it meant. He had been living under the old white supremacist illusion that racism was a form of discrimination or antagonism aimed at a particular racial group. Now we know that racism is actually the system that creates inequality between racial groups and that a racist is anyone who benefits from this system. Obvi. As such, all white people are racist because they all benefit from this system, even if the white person harbors no ill-will against anyone at all.

Anyone with functioning eyeballs saw that the media fueled the unrest with revisionist hallucinations like *The 1619 Project* leading the way in showing how irredeemably racist every aspect of America is. The tag '1619' was a favorite among those woke iconoclasts tearing down statues indiscriminately, even when the figures immortalized actually helped to bring about the end of slavery.

In 2020, an entire anti-racism industry had been propped up to fight the racism that had vanished by the turn of the century but was now in full bloom in large part in order to justify the anti-racism industry. Naturally, the most popular book of 2020 was written by a white woman who earns a 7-figure income going around to colleges and corporate offices to tell other white people that they're racists just for being white.

This year, virtue-signaling became a professional sport. While BLM activists intimidated random people in the street to perform acts of humility on camera, Democrat lawmakers voluntarily knelt to their new wokodoxy, replete with Kente cloths of an African empire that sold and traded slaves.

Meanwhile, professional sports became political comedies. Multi-millionaire athletes used their platform to shame a system that is obviously rigged against people like them making millions of dollars. In an attempt to stay interesting despite the fact that they were playing sit-com games in empty stadiums with cardboard cutout fans and canned cheers, the NBA changed all their jerseys to promote the Marxist Black Lives Matter organization and the NFL expanded the opening ceremonies to give players the opportunity to kneel and show their disgust for the country that makes such protests possible, all the while courting Chinese money by means of ignoring human rights violations in Hong Kong.

Like 2000, 2020 saw a highly contested election surrounded by legal challenges. But, unlike 2000, this year's challenges were brought by the sitting president, and so they were promptly discarded as baseless by the media and government officials across the board. According to the establishment, this was the first election ever that did not have voter fraud and we were all to accept the results, however anomalous they were. We were to accept the notion that a superannuated career politician with record-low enthusiasm could spend the entire election cycle in his basement and still garner 82 million votes. We were to accept the notion that bellwether counties which had predicted the presidency without fail for decades suddenly got it wrong. We were told that a video showing loads of votes being pulled out from under tables and counted multiple times while no partisan observers were present was totally legit because the people who revealed the video said they were in suitcases, not storage containers.

We were told that the election was a referendum on Trump, and so it was. The same people who fought Trump for being sexist promptly quelled accusations of Biden's sexual harassment and ignored clips of the former VP getting fresh with countless girls and young women. The same people who fought Trump for being a racist gleefully voted for Biden, who called Obama "the first sort of mainstream African American who is articulate and bright and clean" and said Latinos were diverse "Unlike the African American community". The same people who pushed to defund the police breathlessly voted for a woman who incarcerated over 1,500 people for marijuana charges and then laughed when she was asked if she ever smoked it, blocked evidence that could have freed an innocent man on death row, and bragged about using felons as cheap labor for the state of California. Anyone who thought they had it rough when Orange Man Bad was in the White House better brace themselves for when Handsy McSniffer and the Butcher of Bakersfield get there.

Our time traveler friend would be most befuddled by how eagerly we traded freedom for safety in 2020. Coming from the decade in which he witnessed the fall of the Soviet Union, it would be unfathomable to him that Americans would so quickly forget that throughout all of modern history the story has been one of people escaping totalitarian collectivist states for free capitalist countries. And yet in 2020 we saw an increasing tendency to push our free capitalist countries toward totalitarian collectivist states. The mantra is familiar: 'This isn't socialism—it's democratic socialism!' And yet the means of oppression and repression are the same. The boot is on the neck even if it's multicolored and glittery.

After the election, America's favorite bartender-congresswoman Alexandria Ocasio-Cortez wondered aloud whether anyone was jotting down the names of those who had supported Trump in case some more industrious types have occasion to dox them or throw them into a concentration camp. When someone informed her that her tweet might come off as a tad bolshie, she added an 'lol'. This isn't totalitarianism—it's lol totalitarianism! Welcome to the '20s.

—December 2020

THE TRIUMPH OF POST-MODERNISM

IT IS COMMONLY SAID THAT a Postmodern culture would be impossible. Anyone who believes that never lived through 2020.

Postmodernism is a philosophy based upon the premise that there is no objective Truth. We have to 'deconstruct' the novel or advertisement or instruction manual and then impose our own meaning to understand it. Consequently, Postmodernists hold that all knowledge is subjective.

That's why most thinkers consider it a nonstarter. If there is no objective Truth, then communication is impossible, and so is all of civilization. If you can't trust that the words before you have a particular meaning, then you cannot trust them at all. That goes for doctor prescriptions as much as for *War and Peace*. As apologist William Lane Craig put it, "Nobody is a postmodernist when it comes to reading the labels on a medicine bottle versus a box of rat poison. If you've got a headache, you'd better believe that texts have objective meaning."

And yet, here we are.

In the year 2020, we have seen the entire world economy shut down over a pathogen that has a 99.7% survival rate. We have seen widespread rioting and looting justified over alleged police racism that accounts for no more than 1.4% of police shootings and likely much less. We have seen the mainstream media and tech companies unabashedly censor the president of the United States of America and many news organizations in the name of democracy. In 2020, we are using rat poisoning to cure a headache. If ever there was a postmodern culture, it is now.

How could this have happened? How could the unworkable intellectual fantasy of Postmodernism actually come to dominate an entire culture?

The answer is that Postmodernism is not really intellectual after all—it is political.

Philosopher Stephen Hicks has shown how Postmodernists developed their theories of epistemological skepticism not as a guide for life or even as academic study but rather as a justification for and undergirding of their political efforts. They knew full well that the principles of Postmodernism were non sequitur. But, it didn't matter as long as they could be used to undermine the politico-economic infrastructure of the West. Liberal Democracy and Capitalism were founded on principles of Individualism, Natural Rights, and Equality before the law, all of which were founded on a belief in and dedication to human Reason. By discrediting Reason, then, the Postmodernists could subvert the entire Western tradition.

This is how the fantastical philosophy became reality. Postmodernists used pedantic boondoggles like Critical Theory to support social constructs such as Systemic Racism, Intersectionality, and Transgenderism. These constructs were then used to prop up policies and initiatives such as Affirmative Action, Subconscious Bias training, and Defund the Police efforts. Finally, these policies crystallized into institutions of government, commerce, and community. It started in academia in the Humanities and Social Sciences and from there metastasized into media, government, business, science, and ultimately into real life.

Like any reified abstraction, it is untrue, but, when people act as if it's true, it exerts a force. GDP growth is not a real thing, but if enough government officials and advisors believe in it, they will craft laws to promote it, and so it will have real consequences on the human beings that make up the economy. Similarly, Postmodernism is a phantom, but, since a significant amount of academics, bureaucrats, and businessmen believe it, it has real consequences.

We see it everywhere in 2020. Of all the 2020-est things, the most 2020-est might have been the racism public health letter that made the rounds in June. Signed by more than a thousand self-professed health professionals, students, and activists, the letter claims that the anti-racism protests that bubbled up after the death of George Floyd did not pose a risk for COVID transmission despite the close interaction of thousands of people. The reason given was that racism and white supremacy are public health concerns in themselves, and so protesting against them is a way to reduce the overall dangers in our society. At the same time, the authors had condemned the previous anti-lockdown protests because they went against public health officials' guidance at the time and because the protests were conducted by mostly white conservatives and so were necessarily racist and therefore a public health risk.

No amount of logic can repair the intellectual havoc this absurdity wreaked. When I first encountered this monstrosity, I thought it must have been a joke. But the letter was being shared by sincere people with advanced degrees. The absurd had become real. Soon after the protests we heard of a spike in COVID cases. But, according to the experts, the spike wasn't due to the protests—it was due to Memorial Day festivities and the anti-lockdown protests, not to the anti-racism protests.

Postmodernism is most ingenious because it cannot be refuted by the standard Western means of argumentation. When normal people encounter Postmodernism in the wild, they will instinctively give its practitioners the benefit of the doubt and attempt to show where the logic broke down somewhere in their reasoning. Of course, as James Lindsey and Helen Pluckrose warn, this is a fool's errand. With Postmodernism, there is no logic to contend with. The enterprise is not founded on Reason at all. On the contrary, it is founded on the abolition of Reason. You can't use Reason to disprove unreason.

This can't end well. Anyone who confronts Postmodernist ideas head-on will eventually find that they lead to coercion and violence. When Reason is forsaken, there can be no civil discourse and there can be no agreement. With Postmodernism, all that is left is power and a Hobbesian struggle of all against all. And, in a year of massive unrest, civil war salvos, and universal moral convulsion, who can deny that is what we see playing out across the public stage?

—December 2020

THE YEAR IDENTITY TRUMPED REALITY

In 2016 we were introduced to the concept of 'fake news'.

In 2017 we didn't need fake news because reality itself had grown so absurd.

The hashtag '#notTheOnion' trended as a way to ensure readers that the outlandish information before them was not meant as satire but rather as a depiction of the new normal.

A handful of examples serves to illustrate: One headline read without a touch of sarcasm that the first ever man gave birth to a baby after being impregnated by a woman.

One article covered a high school girls track meet in which a boy, who was in the middle of transitioning into a girl, competed and won handedly, and the second-place finisher was quoted puzzling over why she felt so out-matched.

Not a few reports were made of teachers and assistants being reprimanded, fined, and even fired for "misgendering" students, or calling them by a gender that they don't identify as.

A Google engineer was fired for violating diversity and inclusion policies after he submitted a memo containing unconventional ideas.

A "deeply progressive" biology teacher at a liberal college in Washington state was denounced as racist and told to resign because he didn't comply with demands that he leave campus for a student-led "Day without Whites".

Several white nationalist conventions saw dozens of several young white men throwing up the 'Roman salute' and shouting "Sieg heil".

The Atlantic Monthly ran a headline pointing out that the Great American Eclipse of 2017 was racist because it passed along a path in which almost no blacks lived.

The sports network ESPN removed an Asian-American commentator named Robert Lee from a game featuring the University of Virginia after concerns that his name would spark outrage from fans troubled by the previous racial tensions in Charlottesville.

An entertainment industry built around sexuality was overcome by reports of sexual harassment and assault from women who made careers off of their sexuality.

College students protested and shut down a panel discussion on free speech because they were afraid the ideas would trigger psychological trauma.

A teacher's assistant at a Canadian arts college was disciplined as intolerant and transphobic for presenting a debate without taking sides.

A *New York Times* op-ed explained that, given psychological effects, speech can be equivalent to violence.

And of course there was Trump. Everything he said seemed to outfake fake news. From a playground taunting match with the North Korean premier to challenging the media to figure out the meaning of his "covfefe" typo, Trump was the perfect leader of post-reality.

And the crazed response from his detractors only spurred him on even more. A group that called themselves 'Antifa', short for 'Anti-fascist', unironically roved around in black masks stealing property, vandalizing, and beating up people they disagreed with.

Indeed, 2017 was the year of the fascist anti-fascists, the fake news that's actually real.

* * *

Disparate as all of these stories seem, there is a unifying theme—in all of these narratives we find that a common understanding of the way the world works has been abandoned for the sake of given individuals' social self-expression. In short, 2017 was the year in which identity trumped reality.

We recognize this theme by the name 'Identity Politics', which has become something of a universal explanation for all of the bizarre things going on in this world. Trump's rise to power? Identity Politics. Police brutality? Identity Politics. Transgenderism? Identity Politics.

At its most basic, Identity Politics seems rather benign and almost natural. Jonathan Rauch defined it as "A political mobilization organized around group characteristics such as race, gender, and sexuality, as opposed to party, ideology, or pecuniary interest." It makes sense—one's group characteristics or 'identity' is important and should be considered in social discourse. Movements such as Abolitionism, Women's Suffrage, and Civil Rights underscore just how firmly planted in our cultural heritage this basic form of Identity Politics is.

But certain forces convened in the mid-20th century that distorted and amplified the premise, ultimately putting us on course for the debacle we see before us. The first is that identity was elevated to the pinnacle of all social, political, and economic concerns, even to the extent of surpassing civic duty, moral obligations, and social cohesion. What started as a compassionate effort to protect the underprivileged and marginalized through charity and grants grew into something of a social and economic juggernaut. Whereas prior to the 1960s people of color and women would try to hide their 'minority' status, afterward they would trumpet it—it could mean scholarship money, grade protection, or government contracts. In this very practical way Identity Politics incentivized differentiation, separation, and uniqueness.

The second force is that a person's identity has become more and more malleable. Coupled with Postmodernist psychologies that questioned the existence of reason and philosophies that questioned the existence of meaning altogether, Identity Politics gave license to people to claim just about any identity that suited them. Gender Theory led the charge. What started as the sensible notion that women were as smart and capable as men grew to become the fantasy that all differences between men and women are social constructs. The charge was to dismantle the social constructs so that women could be as successful as men, but the result was an effort to neglect or destroy any differences at all including patently biological ones. Reality was pushed aside for the sake of identity. It has gotten to a point that a man can compete in female collegiate activities or take a woman-only business loan just because he says he's a woman.

The more influential Identity Politics has become, the more power it has wielded, and the more important it has become for individuals to identify by their group attributes. Even when people don't derive a livelihood from their identity, they derive social esteem or at the very least attention because of it.

Over the course of the mid-century, Identity Politics steadily shifted from a reasonable extension of politics to a ferocious race to annihilate reality. Affirmative Action, Black Power, Gender Studies, Multiculturalism, Intersectionality, Diversity and Inclusion programs, LGBT Rights, and Black Lives Matter by turns intensified the effort.

These days, identity is a person's life, and so it is a matter of depriving one's rights to question that identity. A person should be able to identify as anything he or she wants, even if it contradicts reality. A man says he's a woman? Just fine. A white American says he's a Filippino woman and drives around in a Tuk Tuk? Who are you to judge?

Identity is so dear these day, questioning is tantamount to physical violence. Students have successfully lobbied for a pass on tests because their identity had been threatened; people have lost their jobs for misgendering someone; people claim that their existence is denied because someone disagreed with them.

This is why we have seen a rapid curtailing of freedoms regarding speech and thought in the last several years. It used to be thought that speech was harmless and therefore should be left unbridled; now it is thought that sticks and stones are not the only thing that can hurt you. Identity is a social thing—it necessitates acknowledgment and approval from those around.

And the clearest way of acknowledging and approving is through speech. And so everywhere we see a push to limit what is acceptable and even legal to say. Insults are classed 'hate speech' and hate speech is made punishable by fines or jail time.

Identity Politics tends to grow more frenzied over time by nature—the only way to win is to be different and there is always something else we can do to make ourselves more different. Like a societal Dennis Rodman, we progressively grow more peculiar, more shocking, more repulsive.

So too does it tend to provoke an equally disturbing retaliation in the form of counter-diversity. The increasingly vocal White Supremacist movement in America, as an example, is doubtless a product of the Identity Politics of the last few decades. At least one group has organized a scholarship for underprivileged whites to counter the many other scholarships exclusively for blacks. It makes sense in a twisted way—as long as we're discriminating for scholarships and jobs and contracts, we might as well be equal opportunity discriminators.

And so the vicious cycle continues: Jim Crow begets Affirmative Action, which begets marginalized whites, which begets White Supremacists, which begets a new Jim Crow. Fascists beget anti-fascists, which turn into fascists, and so on. The desperate onlooker wonders whether there can be a way out.

* * *

In an essay titled 'America Wasn't Built for Humans', columnist Andrew Sullivan argues at 'tribalism' is tearing apart our nation. He is basically describing the natural pull of Identity Politics and its destructive tendency in a democratic republic.

While his review of late 20th century fissures is revealing, his premises are wrong. The Founders didn't just "assume we could overcome" tribalism; they confronted it straightaway, building a nation that was capable of handling—nay—taking advantage of the energies inherent in a diverse people. It is not the Founders' negligence that left the door open to tribal unrest but rather the intentional dismantling of the Founders' ideals.

After former ambassador to the U.K. Matthew Barzun returned stateside, he spent time polling U.S. students on what they like and dislike about their country. He said that according to the vast majority of them the most frustrating thing about America today is 'Divisiveness'. When asked what the most positive thing is, the vast majority of them replied 'Diversity'.

What is interesting here is that the two words have the same root and are really two sides of the same concept, which can be summed up as the great American Experiment.

Before Deconstructionists hijacked history departments, it used to be taught that the American Founders envisioned a place where persons of all walks of life could live together in freedom, peace, and prosperity. And for a century and a half the leaders and laymen of this country strove to make that dream a reality. The country was by no means perfect as the record of civil strife clearly shows. But Americans were guided by an ideal and slowly if painstakingly moved toward that vision.

The ideal was founded on the simple principle that "all men are created equal". The Declaration of Independence established it, the Constitution enshrined it, and great leaders from Jefferson to Garrison to King found it the lodestar for their work. It did not mean that all men were created without differences, but rather that through right reason they could look past their differences and connect with all other men. To the founders, one's identity as a human person is based in something that everyone shared—that is what is to be focused on and that is what can allow such a variety of peoples to coexist in freedom, peace, and prosperity.

And this is the key—tribalism wasn't sidestepped accidentally; tribalism was held at bay because the Founders intentionally built this country on the principle of sameness under God. Now, the powers that be have refashioned the country around the principle differentness before others. We have traded the Founders' identity based in reason for a Postmodernist identity based in whimsy.

Thus we find ourselves in an Orwellian world where children are leaders, modesty is rape, and truth is lies. If we are to overcome our tribalism and unite as it was once thought possible, we must give up the new concept of identity and retrieve the former concept. And to do that we must first recall what it is at the very core of identity in the first place and what it means to be human.

—December 2017

THE
RIFT

EVERYTHING IS A BLUE/ BLACK WHITE/ GOLD DRESS AND IT'S TEARING US APART

DO YOU TRUST THE ELECTION system? Chances are, if you're a Democrat, you do, and, if you're a Republican, you don't. A new poll found that 90% of Democrats thought that the 2020 presidential election was free and fair while an astounding 70% of Republicans didn't. Same event; completely opposite perceptions. One must wonder whether they are even looking at the same thing.

In a way, they aren't.

Ask a Democrat about the election and he is likely to praise the record number of voters and the victory of the first woman Vice President candidate as a testament to American Democracy. Ask a Republican about the election and he is likely to lament over the inconsistent vote-counting procedures and fraud allegations as signs of third-world-style corruption.

Of course, four years ago, things were rather reversed. After the 2016 election, it was the Democrats who were fearful of the irregularities and alleging malfeasance while the Republicans were busy celebrating the American electoral system. It seems every major election is seen completely differently depending upon who you're talking to.

And it's not just the elections that cause the divergent views. Every major event this year has been viewed as completely different by those on the Left and those on the Right: The Coronavirus Pandemic and government lockdowns, the BLM protests and riots, the Trump impeachment, the Jeffrey Epstein scandal, the wildfires and climate change, and the confirmation of Amy Coney Barrett to the Supreme Court.

On any of these or countless other issues of the day, you will likely get an opposite report from those who consider themselves modern liberals and those who consider themselves conservatives. Each will firmly believe that they are seeing things correctly and that the other side has got it all wrong.

A meme making the rounds summarizes perfectly. Ron Swanson is being asked if his family has a history of mental illness. He responds "I have an uncle who thinks right wing agitators were the ones actually causing the riots and not Antifa and BLM." It's funny because it's true.

But it's also funny because it's false. His uncle probably thinks he is crazy for thinking and BLM are causing the riots. There are those who don't even think there are riots going on at all. To them, the thought of Portland conjures images, not of lawless mobs terrorizing retailers, but of people swaying with candles in the night singing 'Kumbaya'.

The assumption is that there is one thing to see, and anyone who doesn't see it the same way is either crazy or intentionally lying. Time to unfriend anyone who seriously believes the conspiracy theory that there is voter fraud going on in the United States! (At least until your candidate loses.)

But what if they aren't actually crazy or lying? What if something else is going on?

BLUE AND BLACK OR WHITE AND GOLD

In early 2015, Scottish singer Caitlyn McNeill posted a picture of a dress and asked the Internet to help her decide what color it was—blue and black or white and gold. Then all hell broke loose. The response she got quickly brewed into a worldwide controversy as everyone chimed in with his opinion. Strangely, half of the people saw blue and black and the other half saw white and gold.

The thing is, everyone was adamant. Those who saw blue and black were certain that it was blue and black and couldn't understand how people saw white and gold. Taylor Swift posted "I don't understand this odd dress debate and I feel like it's a trick somehow. I'm confused and scared. PS it's OBVIOUSLY BLUE AND BLACK." But those who saw white and gold felt the same way. It was obvious to them and they couldn't believe anyone else saw it differently.

A few years after the dress debate, a strange audio clip started making the rounds and provided a similar controversy. Was it saying 'Yanni' or 'Laurel'? Half heard the former, half the latter. It was even more puzzling than the dress dust up because the audio seems so much more precise. How can someone hear an 'L' sound when someone else hears a 'Y'? It seems psychically impossible.

The reason this happens is that one's perception of the sound is based upon the way his or her aural receptors are formed. For some, their receptors are tuned to a higher pitch so that they don't hear lower frequencies as much. Others are tuned to a lower pitch so that they don't hear treble sounds as much. The Yanni/Laurel clip is so controversial because the sound is played right in the middle of the spectrum so that lower-frequency hearers experience one thing and higher-frequency hearers experience another.

The Yanni/Laurel clip shows us that everyone experiences life from different perspectives. People are quite literally tuned to hear different things, to experience life differently, even if the reality is the same for all.

The dress illusion has a similar explanation. While the object we're looking at has definite attributes, we experience those attributes in different ways. The dress in question was in reality a black and blue sequined dress. But, in the picture, the light distorted the hues of the colors so it actually appears white and gold. Those who judge what they see directly will likely see it as white and gold while those who are judging what they think the colors are in real life will translate their sensory perception so that they see black and blue.

Both of these illusions present what philosophers will call a 'dispective'. Though there is a single reality, our different perspectives make us experience it in different ways. Since our experiences are so intimate, we think that it is the only possible way that anyone could see reality—indeed, to us, experience is reality. Hence the befuddlement when someone actually sees it differently. Surely, they are blind or being willfully ignorant.

And yet, one's experience, true as it might seem, is only one slice of reality that others might well not share. A thought experiment drives the point home. To play, simply say how many words are in the box below.

```
┌─────────────────────────────────┐
│                                 │
│         THE     THE             │
│                                 │
└─────────────────────────────────┘
```

You might say that it is obvious that there are two words because, of course, there are two instances of the word 'THE'. And it is so obvious that anyone who thinks otherwise must be blind or willfully ignorant. But others will say that there are two instances of one word and so the answer to the question is that there is only one word in the box—the word 'THE'. Anyone who thinks otherwise is either blind or willfully ignorant.

In fact, either answer is correct depending upon how you look at the question. There are two words and there is only one. The audio clip plays both 'Yanni' and 'Laurel'. The dress is black and blue and at the same time white and gold.

Now, these controversies can be the source of delightful diversion as in the case of the dress or a quirky audio clip. But in the case of our political debates this phenomenon has led to severe conflict, violence, and strife that some pundits argue could lead to civil war.

OUR BLUE/BLACK WHITE/GOLD WORLD

Today, everything is a Blue/Black White/Gold Dress phenomenon. From the Coronavirus Pandemic to the BLM protests to the elections, every news story and every public controversy takes the same form: One side sees it one way and can't imagine anyone seeing it another way while the other side sees it completely differently and likewise thinks other side is crazy for not seeing it the way they do.

The fact is, people are made of different stuff, so experiencing an event or issue will produce vastly different experiences. We are tuned to different frequencies, and, as it appears, about half are tuned to the Left and the other half tuned to the Right. In the same way that our sense receptors are tuned to hear higher or lower pitches, our socio-political worldviews are shaped in a way that distort objective reality into vastly different experiences.

Of course, this is nothing new. Human beings have always had different perspectives—we've always been tuned to different frequencies. What we've seen in recent years is an increase in constructs that amplify our tuning one way or another. To understand fully would require a sizable effort. Suffice it to say that our social age makes politics more important than ever. Increasingly, a win for one must mean loss for the other side. Social media and echo chambers have only exacerbated an already tenuous situation to the extent that many pundits fear civil war.

In a 1960 presidential debate, Richard Nixon said that he and his opponent John F. Kennedy agreed on the end goal, and they just disagree on how to get there. Watching the elections this year, it would be unfathomable for anyone from either party to say such a thing. To pretty much everyone on both sides, this election represents an existential battle, where the good side (our side) must prevail lest we fall into the abyss of the other side's darkness.

Granted, this is hyperbole. But there are sincere people on both sides who firmly hold these beliefs. They are tuned to irreconcilable frequencies and are experiencing life in completely different ways. If we stand a chance, it is by first acknowledging that people see things differently and recognizing that it doesn't make them crazy.

—November 2020

THE
DIVERSITY
PROBLEM

Lykewyse is a startup based out of San Antonio, TX, offering an assortment of personal assistant apps. In hopes of hitting the big time with a new grocery app, the leadership team pulled out all the stops. They hired the best tech and management personnel in the industry and did all the necessary market research. They weren't satisfied with riding the wave with this app—they wanted to lead the way with it.

But they had a problem.

Despite the fact that their market was primarily women and a mix of ethnicities, their leadership team was 100% white and male. They had the technical expertise but not the cultural understanding to really succeed. As the CEO put it, they were "at severe risk of making boneheaded mistakes" because they were out of touch with their customers. They needed to be more diverse.

And so they set out to make their leadership look more like their customers. They had to let go of several otherwise qualified leaders to make room for women and people of color. As they saw it, they had to do it. If they didn't think like their clients, they were history.

After bringing in many big-name women and people of color, the company touted one of the most diverse leadership teams in tech, and boasted that they had the widest range of perspective to make the right decisions. They made some key changes to the design and marketing, and readied the app to ship.

On launch day, spirits were high. At first. The numbers were low from the start. And by the time the initial campaign was over, they had sold about 25 percent the number they had planned for. Something somewhere went astray.

As it turns out, the app wasn't intuitive to the users, mainly women who shop. They didn't want to have to switch back and forth between apps; they wanted the content to be integrated. The Lykewyse app, largely due to changes made because of the new leadership, was cumbersome and not user-friendly. Of course, these were exactly the kind of "boneheaded mistakes" that they sought to avoid by bringing on a more diverse team. How in the world did they get it wrong?

Breaking down the app in their retrospective, they attempted to under-stand what had happened. One of the men asked one of the women leaders if she used it when she went shopping. There was silence. "I don't go grocery shopping," she said, and then looked to the other women. None of them really did the shopping either. It was their husband who did the shopping, or they ate out all the time, but none ever did the kind of shopping that the app was designed for.

And then it hit them. The women were brought on to make their leadership team more diverse, but they had failed to add the perspective that was most crucial to their success—that of their female customers. How could this have possibly happened?

* * *

Below is a list of demographics. Read them and guess which celebrity it refers to.

Born in 1948 in Great Britain
Male
White
Married and remarried
At least two children
Net worth greater than $220 million
Likes dogs, sports cars, fine wines, and traveling

If you guessed Prince Charles, you are wrong. The correct answer is Ozzy Osbourne. Actually, these data match both Ozzy Osbourne and Prince Charles, but I was thinking particularly about the Oz, so you lose.

That is a mean trick, I know. I play it to point out an important fact: Demographics can mislead. Looking at the stats, it's clear that the Oz and Ol' Chuck have an uncanny amount in common, but you're not going to advertise to them with the same image; you're not going to talk to them in the same way; and you're not going to sell them the same product. If you go strictly by demographics, you may very well skew your message in the wrong direction. You might be pushing plaid golf knickers when your customer might be more interested in black eyeliner and bat feeders.

Consider the story of Lykewyse. Their move toward a more diverse leadership team made sense on the surface—they wanted to think more like their customers. As it turned out, they were looking at demographics which didn't help them as it should have and ultimately might have hurt them.

Their case is not out of the ordinary. They wanted to make their leadership team more like their target customers. But they boiled their customers down to a few demographic categories and called it a day. Their customers were women, so they wanted to bring on more women leaders. But the women that they brought on weren't the same kind of women that comprised their market. Their market consisted in middle-class, family-oriented mothers; their new leaders were more independent than those in their market, more career-oriented, and more technical as most had established themselves in the startup environment. None of these characteristics are easy to quantify, so they couldn't use them when deciding whom to hire. And yet, ultimately, those characteristics were enough to set them apart from their market and hinder them from providing the key perspective.

* * *

These days, everyone's bonkers over diversity. No matter what the question is, it is just assumed that diversity is the answer. Need to stay relevant with customers? Diversity! Big product launch coming up? Diversity! Want to innovate to stay ahead of the game? Diversity!

There is good reason: The more diverse our group is, the more angles on the truth we will have and the closer to full understanding we can get.

Recall the six blind men in the Indian traditional who all describe an elephant differently based on which part of the beast they can touch. One touches the trunk and says the elephant is like a snake; another touches the ear and says it's like a fan; another touches the leg and says it's like a tree. The fact is they must combine their perspectives to fully understand what the elephant is like.

Truth is like an elephant, and we are like the six blind men. The more perspectives we can amass, the fuller our picture of the truth, the better our decisions, and the greater our success will be.

As such, companies are falling over themselves to instate diversity and inclusion programs. HR departments emphasize diversity and inclusion through compliance courses; so called 'diversity business groups' give different types of people a place to connect; and diversity fairs give folks a chance to learn about and experience a variety of cultures.

There's only one problem in all of this hyperventilating: We don't know what diversity is.

If you Google the word 'diversity', you'll get a picture of a group of people with different skin colors, a mix of men and women, and possibly a variety of ages. To the typical American, this is diversity. It is what diversity looks like in government, universities, the media, and corporate America, and if you have it you have diversity. In fact, when companies are rated on diversity, they look at only two metrics: skin color and gender. For all intents and purposes, this is the extent of diversity.

But what don't we see in that picture? We don't see different cultures (all are clearly Western); we don't see different styles (all are business casual);

and we don't see any ugly people (because these are all models for a stock photography shoot). To be sure, we don't see differing religions, politics, or philosophies because there is no reliable way of capturing those differences in an image—the way one thinks is not visible.

As it is with the startup Lykewyse and our Ozzy/Prince Charles thought experiment, viewing diversity in this way is limiting and possibly misleading.

This conception of diversity is more troubling than it might seem: By defining diversity as a mix of skin color and gender, we make it very visual, and, by making it visual, we make it base. The assumption is that, if we have different skin colors or genders, we come from different places, and, if we come from different places, we must think differently and thus provide something different to the team.

Did you notice what happened there? By making diversity visual, we are forced to prejudge a person's character based on very superficial things. Far from empowering or enlightening, this smacks of the kind of mentality that proponents of diversity and inclusion fought against in the 1950s and '60s.

In perhaps the most powerful line of rhetoric of all time, Martin Luther King asserted: "I have a dream that my four children will be judged, not by the color of their skin, but by the content of their character." Now, largely due to the policies that his followers instituted, content of character is determined to be the result of skin color, and so the only way to judge someone's character is by his skin color.

There can be no doubt that visual measures are convenient. So too are they powerful. Of all our senses, the visual is the one from which we derive the most information by far—10 million pieces of information per second comes from our visual senses compared to 1 million for auditory and fewer for the other senses. If you want to make an impact, you want to make it visual.

But, as we have seen, when diversity is made a visual matter, it becomes superficial and base. If an HR manager says that we need a certain number of employees with a certain skin color or gender, he is saying that their skin color or gender must determine who they are to some extent, and thus dictate what they provide to the company. Isn't that exactly what the diversity and inclusion initiatives are trying to fight against?

The problem with our understanding of diversity is that it is visual and thus limited and dangerous. If we are to support a true diversity, we need to go deeper.

A Better Kind of Diversity

If we think about it, the goal of diversity is to secure a variety of perspectives. Yes, a different skin color and gender might mean that you have had different experiences and thus that you could provide different perspectives. But that isn't always guaranteed—sometimes two people with different genders might have the exact same background and thus provide similar perspectives, just as it was in the Lykewyse example. By the same token, people with the same skin color or gender could have had vastly different experiences and thus arrive at divergent perspectives, just as it was with Prince Charles and Ozzy.

What is most important in all of this is perspective. And, if we hope to provide a truly diverse environment, we have to take into account not just different superficial characteristics, but different ways of viewing the world.

I once had the meaning of perspective explained to me by an eight-year-old girl. I was traveling on a train, and, nearing the station, the passengers were all moving toward the exit. A family gathered by the door, mother, father, a girl, and her younger brother. Each was carrying a huge amount of luggage and the little boy was struggling. He let out a moan: "This bag is too big!" Without missing a beat, the girl said, "No, you're just too small!"

Perspective is the way you look at something, the mental tools in your box with which you decipher, understand, and interact with the world around you. We all have different tools, which are reflected in how we approach the various scenarios we deal with. The little boy was viewing things subjectively—what did he as a boy want at this moment? The little girl was viewing things objectively—what was it that the family was trying to accomplish and what was needed from each family member to get there? It was the same situation, but two different perspectives.

We see the same kind of mental flipping throughout our culture. Consider the great thinker Michel de Montaigne, who, while playing with a cat wondered whether the cat was not really playing with him. Or consider the spiritual saying: Instead of telling God how big our problems are, let's start telling our problems how big our God is. Perspective allows us to view the world from multiple angles, to get a fuller picture of the truth before us so as to make the best decisions. Diverse perspectives are good. The question is, how do we ensure the most diverse perspectives?

It turns out, most people have a well-founded perspective based on how they think and act. Everyone has preferences and so everyone has an approach to life that can be utilized in these kinds of situations. Altogether, a person's approach to life amounts to what might be rightly called 'personality'—the combination of traits and qualities that form an individual's distinctive character. It is personality that makes us each unique, personality that drives our thoughts and action, and personality that people see when they get to know us.

And herein lies the solution to the diversity problem. In order to get a fuller picture of the truth, we need diversity, not of skin color or gender, but of personalities. If we can identify everyone's personality, we can better understand how they would think and act given different situations, we can better assemble and arrange groups, and we can use this framework as a tool to better interact with those who differ. Achieving diversity, then, is a matter not of measuring and categorizing based on skin color or gender, but rather based on personality type.

* * *

Studies show that displaying brain scans automatically increases credibility even if the scans are completely irrelevant to the subject. Accordingly, here is a scan of two brains:

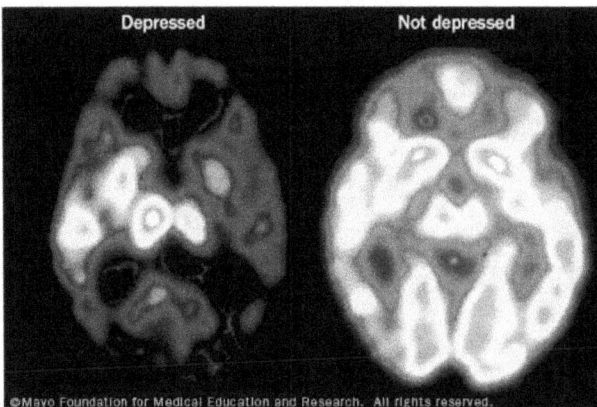

Aren't you convinced?

Joking aside, what this shows is that two different brains react in different ways given the same stimuli. In other words, people see, digest, and think about things differently depending upon their brain constitution, their temperament, their personality.

Fortunately, we don't have to all wear portable FMRI machines to understand our personalities. There is a less cumbersome and still reliable way of measuring the way a person thinks—a personality test. The idea of a personality test is simple: Ask the subject about his preferences, consolidate the answers into a type, and derive tendencies and correlations from it.

There is a whole suite of such tests including 'Strengths Finder', 'Color Code', 'Big Five', 'Enneagram', and the inimitable 'Which Furby Are You?'. And, while all have their charms, the 'Myers-Briggs Type Indicator' or 'MBTI' stands out as the best.

First, the Myers-Briggs test is based on the serious work of Carl Jung, whose 1923 book Psychological Types served as a watershed in under-standing personalities. Jung mapped out eight archetypes based on three axes, providing the groundwork Myers-Briggs' sixteen types on four axes. Altogether, the framework provides a comprehensive view of an individual's tastes and inclinations.

Second, MBTI is time-tested, being formulated by the mother-daughter team of Katharine Cook Briggs and Isabel Briggs Myers as early as the 1910s, and finalized for widespread use by the Second World War. It has since been the industry standard and consequently there are plenty of data to work with.

While the MBTI doesn't provide the fidelity that a portable FMRI might, it is remarkably accurate and stands as a dynamic tool for a number of purposes, not the least of which is today's breathless quest for diversity. As a way to identify various perspectives and a framework with which to synthesize them, the Myers-Briggs method is peerless.

Consider our Lykewyse example. In their effort to provide more diversity, the leadership team sought more women and people of color. As it turned out, their diverse recruits all saw the world in the same way that their precursors did and so failed to provide the perspective necessary to avoid disaster.

If the team had looked beyond the surface to personality traits, things might have turned out differently. They could have measured the way each person interacted socially, how they took in information, processed it, and made use of it. By administering the MBTI or some other personality test, the leadership team could have gained insights into their strengths and weaknesses, thus giving them the tools to capitalize on their fortes and beef up the areas where they were lacking. They could have compared it to their target market so as to better understand how their customers perceived and processed the world.

Diversity is one area in which personality type thinking can be of service. Taking a step back, we find that this concept can be applied to all realms of our lives: school, work, politics, romance—you name it. Personality thinking is relevant in everything we do because it is crucial to understanding the way we think, act, and interact with others.

—August 2017

THE MYTH OF DIVISIVENESS

As the final poll numbers came in over the weekend and news outlets began declaring Joe Biden victor of the 2020 presidential election, the response was nearly uniform: Biden's win meant the end to the most divisive presidency in American history. Now would start a new era of peace and unity.

I thought this strange considering practically half of the country voted against Biden. It seems to me that we're awfully divided no matter who is president. That didn't occur to the ecstatic media, who saw Trump as so divisive that anyone who replaced him would be a force for unity. With Trump we couldn't possibly come together. Without him, anything was possible.

But this wasn't the first time we had heard this.

Déjà Vu

In fact, the same narrative was rolled out in 2008 after Barack Obama had defeated John McCain. You might remember. At that time it was George W. Bush who had divided our country and a new dawn was rising of unity and peace under Obama.

Looking back, we find that we heard the same story in 1992, when George H. W. Bush had divided the nation and Bill Clinton was going to unite us once again. In fact, it wasn't just Trump who was seen as divisive, it was every Republican president going back to Nixon. And it's not just Biden who is going to bring us peace and unity. It's every Democratic president back to Kennedy. What exactly is going on here?

To be sure, it might well be that Republican leaders are in fact divisive while Democratic presidents are not. With the Bushes, there were highly contentious wars. With Nixon, there was Watergate. With Trump, there were no more new wars, but there was that whole Russian interference thing and his bluster speaks for itself. Perhaps Republicans are just divisive by nature.

But the theory doesn't pass muster. Democrats have done and said some very divisive things as well. In addition to their wars and contentious policies, their rhetoric has been especially incendiary. One analyst called Obama the most divisive president in American history.

Why don't we hear about that? There's a simple answer. A person is only seen as divisive if we disagree with him. If we agree with what a person says and stands for, he cannot be divisive. It just so happens that the people who determine who's divisive and who's not all agree with what the Democrats say and they don't agree with what the Republicans say. So Republicans are divisive and Democrats unite.

United By Division

The myth is that only one side is divisive. If we listen to the media, a Biden presidency will mean that all disagreement will suddenly end, that Democrats and Republicans will hold hands, and everyone will be singing 'Kumbaya' in the streets. Of course this is nonsense. The policies that Democrats have promised to install will be just as divisive as anything Trump has done. And the rhetoric is possibly more divisive now that the DNC has adopted the intersectional playbook of the social justice warriors. Biden and Harris-led Democrats paint half of the country as racist and sexist—can you get more divisive than that? The critical difference is that the big-tech-media-industrial-complex agrees with them, and so there won't be a chorus weeping and wailing about how divisive they're being.

Every president is divisive inasmuch as we have a divided country. As long as we are split down the middle on every major issue, any president who has an ounce of conviction will be divisive. But that's not the way it's portrayed in the media. Only one side is divisive and the other, by default, is unifying.

It's really a brilliant trick. You can't defend against the accusation of being divisive. If you deny it, you prove them right by being divisive. It's like if someone called you argumentative. What are you supposed to do? If you deny it, you prove them right by arguing. But if you're agreeable, you accept the label and so you're argumentative anyway.

There's no escape from this catch, as Trump has woefully discovered. Like an unwearied Sisyphus, Trump can push the boulder up the hill only to have the gods push it back down again.

Divided We Stand

Yes, this nation is divided after four years of Trump. But it was divided after eight years of Obama too. Those in the media see the sharp divide and point to Trump—he caused this! In reality, it could have been anybody not a Democrat in the White House and the accusations would have been the same. Thanks to the media, everyone knows that Trump is literally Hitler. But I remember propaganda that painted George W. Bush, John McCain, and Mitt Romney as Hitler too. Everyone who opposes the Left is literally Hitler.

It just so happens that Trump doesn't back down when he is taunted. He keeps fighting—pushing the boulder up the hill. He may be stubborn and even childish to keep trying. But he shouldn't be considered divisive. He's just standing his ground. And with all the garbage that has been thrown at him over the last four years, that is an impressive feat in itself.

—November 2020

HOW TO DISAGREE: THREE RULES TO MAKE THE MOST OF OUR DIVISIVENESS

THERE IS A RULE THAT you should never talk about politics or religion in polite company. I've never been a fan.

What else is worth talking about? And, really, is it even possible to talk about anything these days and not get into politics and religion?

Consider the go-to non-controversial topic—the weather. How far can you get in a conversation about the weather without stumbling upon climate change and thus politics? As Orwell pointed out, "In our age there is no such thing as 'keeping out of politics.' All issues are political issues, and politics itself is a mass of lies, evasions, folly, hatred and schizophrenia."

The problem of course is that religion and politics cause disagreement, and nobody knows how to disagree. The SNL dinner party skit would be funny if it weren't so awkwardly true. Disagreement has always been tricky, and even more so in the age of Internet trolls and SJW witch hunts. The wrong word and you could lose your job or worse you could be unfriended in social media. Nowadays, disagreement is a dangerous business.

This is a shame because it generates a chilling effect on conversation and hinders intellectual growth. For all its faults, disagreement can be constructive if done properly. We gain new insights, learn, and problem solve through good disagreement.

More importantly, however, disagreement can help us connect in a way that disingenuous superficial agreement never can. We can all agree that we live in fairly uncivilized times. But it's not lack of community that has caused us to disagree so; it's our lack of good disagreement that has broken up our community. Paradoxically, one could say that disagreeing could make us more not less civil.

So, instead of avoiding religion and politics at dinner parties, I propose we just learn how to disagree better. We don't have time for any Monty Python Argument Clinic nonsense. We want good, solid argument. Realizing it's a little optimistic, I hold out hope. Accordingly, here are three rules that will help get us there:

1. Don't take it personally—just because I disagree with you doesn't mean I hate you. It means I disagree with you.

Last year, the Boy Scouts announced they would allow girls into their ranks. After someone posted a story on it, I suggested that the Boy Scouts would have to change their name since it wasn't just for boys anymore.

This might have been a reasonable statement in times past, but, in the twenty-teens, it is tantamount to genocide. The insults and cursing came out, all-caps were unleashed—it was social media war.

One person said that because of my statement I was denying his existence. By simply making a semantic distinction, I had been guilty of preventing him from existing.

Now, I can appreciate a powerful analogy. He had apparently aligned himself with an ideology that celebrated the gender fluidity of the Boy Scouts decision. By questioning the logic of the decision, I was questioning the guy's ideology and perhaps his most cherished affiliations and constructs. To him it might have seemed as though I was trying to deny his existence.

But he wasn't being figurative. To him, like so many in our modern world, his ideology had become his life, and so questioning it had in a very real sense become a kind of death.

This is the new normal. In a social age such as ours, we become our groups, affiliations, and identities. When someone questions or harms those groups, affiliations, or identities, it is as though they are doing harm to us personally. These days, disagreeing is an existential threat.

There is some validity to this thinking. One's thoughts and beliefs can and do affect one's actions, and actions in our political climate can affect the lives of others. A person says he's conservative, and conservatives vote for Trump, who could very well thrust us into World War III. The conclusion is that the conservative's beliefs could bring about the end of the world, and so he must be censured as if the world depended upon it.

While this mentality is sensibly laid out as such, we can easily see how it goes too far. The term 'conservative' has many meanings, not all conservatives voted for Trump, and we don't know for sure that Trump is going to start World War III anyway. No matter. You're either with us or against us, and, if you're against us, you're literally Hitler.

The disagreement might be on the tax rate or school vouchers, but, given the kind of existential angst we're dealing with, we're compelled to disavow the other and likely shout him down. We even might feel at liberty to punch him or steal from him because of course that's the only way to deal with Nazis.

We have fallen into the trap of 'concept creep'. One fault or flaw seamlessly blends into another more heinous offense. A sexist remark is rape; acknowledging differences between ethnicities is racism; disagreeing with someone is hate and hate is violence.

Mark Lilla pointed out how modern liberals found success making the fight for civil rights a moral issue, and ultimately winning on the moral high ground. As he put it, "It got liberals into the habit of treating every issue as one of inviolable right, leaving no room for negotiation, and inevitably cast opponents as immoral monsters rather than simply as fellow citizens with different views."

And, certainly, taking this stance makes our case more emphatic, and grants us moral authority in some cases. But, after all, it is a logical fallacy, and ultimately prevents civil disagreement from taking place.

Don't take it personally—just because I disagree with you doesn't mean I hate you.

2. Come from curious—it is the wisest man who knows he knows nothing.

In her TED Talk On Being Wrong Kathryn Schultz outlines the typical thought process when one comes across someone with an opposing view.

First, we start with the Ignorance Assumption, where we think that the other is ignorant, and just unload all of the information that we have on the topic. Surely that will make them see the light.

When they don't get it, we move onto the Idiocy Assumption, where we surmise that the other is incapable of making a sound judgment at all. This is where ridicule, insults, and all-caps come into play.

Then, when they still don't get it, we move to the Evil Assumption, where it's pretty clear the other is just malicious and out to destroy the world. This is where the claims of racism, sexism, xenophobia, etc. come into play. Clearly, if after all of that, they still don't agree, they must want to destroy the world.

Or it could be that they have a different perspective than we do, and might actually be right. We shudder to think.

There was once in conversation, long before we banished dialectic from the public sphere, a technique called the Socratic Method. The idea is that two could arrive at the truth by asking questions. Someone would make a claim and Socrates would follow with clarifying questions until they arrived at an agreement, usually quite different from the original statement.

These days, we don't ask questions. And if we do ask questions we do so as a way to set up the other in a kind of trap. And so even when people ask questions no one answers them. Socrates would not be impressed.

The key is that we must be sincere about the questions we ask. Learn more about the other's perspective, and be open to the possibility that we are wrong, or at least that the other is not wrong. They too have good insights and it's quite possible we can learn from them.

Granted, they might be wrong after all. There is a reason why you disagree. But chances are sincere questions can help you see the matter from a new perspective and possibly help you find common ground.

Come from curious—it is the wisest man who knows he knows nothing.

3. MAKE STEEL MEN—IT SERVES NO ONE TO DEFEAT THE STRAW MAN.

In Jordan Peterson's now infamous showdown with the BBC's Cathy Newman, the host was shown repeatedly badgering Peterson with false representations of his statements. Peterson would say something, then Newman would reply, "So you're saying…" and then completely distort what he had said into something ridiculous or contemptible.

The tactic is familiar to anyone who engages in debates these days—it is the logical fallacy of the Straw Man. In short, the idea is to frame your opponent's argument in a way that is exaggerated, implausible, or otherwise faulty so that you can then knock it over like a man made of straw.

It's especially pernicious in a heated debate because the adept arguer can and often does lure their victim in with a somewhat reasonable claim—something that isn't too far from what they really would say. But then, once he subscribes to it, they will point out the ridiculous part and tear down the whole thing. They are crowned victor and it's almost impossible to recover.

It takes an ultra-conscientious thinker like Peterson to stop the Straw Man before it is propped up. Meanwhile, the technique persists nonetheless and continues to confound interlocutors and degrade dialogue everywhere.

But the Straw Man is cheap, and only divides. As Andrew Lang asserted, "No gentleman ever consciously misrepresents the ideas of an opponent." It is a mark of our age that hardly anyone these days argues without misrepresenting the ideas of their opponents.

If we are to improve the quality of discussion and, dare I say, disagreement, we must replace the Straw Man with his noble cousin, the Steel Man. Instead of repeating your opponent's argument to make it sound flimsy and silly, make it sound bold and powerful. Try to make it better than your opponent made it, and then try to defeat it. Only then will you know that you are on the side of truth.

It's possible that you can't defeat it after all, and that'd be a good thing because you have a more well-rounded view of the truth as a result.

Charlie Munger took it to the extreme: "I'm not entitled to have an opinion unless I can state the arguments against my position better than the people who are in opposition."

If everyone used this policy to govern their interaction, we'd have a lot less conflict and a lot more productivity. Make steel men—it serves no one to defeat the straw man.

I submit these knowing well how unlikely it is that they will overcome the pressures of our social age and reinstate a kind of civility in our discourse. But, at the very least, it might help prove that it is possible to have a civil disagreement. And hopefully people won't be so inclined to run away when politics and religion come up at the next dinner party.

—March 2018

THE
ERR

FAKE NEWS ISN'T THE PROBLEM, RELATIVISM IS

WHEN THE SOON-TO-BE-PRESIDENT Trump called a CNN reporter 'fake news' to his face, it was both entertaining and ironic. First of all, it was great theater seeing such an esteemed agency being called out in such a public forum. But, if anyone is a peddler of fake news, it is Trump.

Fake news has become something of a boogeyman man of late. Since Trump's surprising election, politicians and pundits from both sides of the debate have pointed to fake news as a major culprit in the debacle.

But so-called fake news is not limited to news agencies broadcasting dubious partisan views—that is just the most prominent example, so everyone, including the future president, is harping on it. Looking closer, we see that fake news actually stems from a more fundamental crisis of philosophy that has swept through our culture in the last decades: The belief that truth is relative and all one needs to do to make something true is to say it. That philosophy is what fake news is all about, and the Donald might be its most reliable adherent.

The Post-Truth Era.

Ever since the election, pundits and sore loser Hillary supporters have been up in arms. The idea is that new media organizations spread articles, clips, and memes full of falsehoods and fallacies that persuade vast contingents of people to believe some blatantly wrong things. Because it's all framed as real news, people consume it, believe it, and share it, thus spreading the fakery to all corners of society, sometimes outpacing and overshadowing what might be called 'real news'.

As a result, fake news has been blamed for all kinds of wild widespread beliefs and many suggest that fake news is the cause of criminal or otherwise regrettable behavior. Not a few pundits blamed fake news for the surprise 2016 presidential election. From polls that claimed Clinton had a safe lead going into the election to bizarre stories that said Pope Francis endorsed Trump, fake news seemed to guide the election throughout. Post-election, critics have pounced on White House representatives KellyAnne Conway for suggesting that they could use "alternative facts" and Sean Spicer for saying that "sometimes we disagree with the facts".

It has gotten to the point that critics have called this the 'Post-Truth Era'.

In response, the outcry has been swift and fierce. The pejorative 'fake news' has been slung around as a way to discredit questionable agencies, an effort that our bombastic president has eagerly joined in on. Meanwhile,

Facebook execs pledged to cut down on the fake news sites that disseminate through their social network. And many reputable sources have released nifty how-to guides for determining the difference between real and fake news.

Of course, none of this seems to be making an impact. After two months of disclaiming fake news and vowing to stick to the truth, we see the same fallacious arguments and dubious sources being flung about as if nothing has changed.

A recent incident is telling: On the day of the inauguration, the IT outlet Techcrunch ran a story on how to mitigate fake news, but the very same day it also ran a widely shared article on how the LGBT rights page had disappeared from the White House site, insinuating that the new Trump administration had immediately begun a campaign to deprive citizens of their rights.

Now, anyone with a basic understanding of politics knows that, during every inauguration, the government removes the previous administration's policy information from the White House site. The page that Techcrunch called the 'LGBT rights page' was actually just an article championing Obama's support of the LGBT community and featured a picture of the former president signing a law with a bunch of gay people around him. There would be no reason for Trump to keep the page up no matter what the custom was. And, yet, Techcrunch saw it fit to rage about how the Trump era was already hindering progress that was so diligently fought for during the last eight years. This was by all accounts a fake news article. And it permeated the ether with the best of them.

It would seem that Techcrunch, like pretty much every other media outlet around these days, just cannot put down the fake news habit. Even when they acknowledge the problem and dedicate time and effort to stopping it, they continue to disseminate it. And, all the while, falsehoods and fallacies continue to swarm around unhindered.

One wonders whether those trying to put an end to fake news really know what it is they're supposed to be fighting. The caricature painted is of a group of unkempt political hacks in some basement cooking up the most malicious plot to sway the public mind. This is the mentality that has led to the conspiracy theory that Russia hacked the election.

When we look into it, we find that the reality is far from it. Sometimes it is just careless speculation that gives birth to the fake news; sometimes it is earnest good intention that leads us down the wrong path. In any case, it cannot be assumed that some vicious Russian hacker is guilty—the forces that have led us to this point are pervasive, and all sides of a given argument are affected. As the inimitable Pogo said, "We have seen the enemy and he is us."

And so it will be constructive to pick apart this strange new phenomenon in hopes of better understanding it and ultimately combating it. What is fake news? How is it so successful? And why is it so difficult to eradicate? As we analyze, we find that it's not so strange and new after all.

FAKE NEWS ROOKERY.

Fake news is not news. It has been around at least since Mark Antony and Caesar Augustus fought a disinformation campaign against each other for the Empire. What's changed is the ability for fake news to spread and the willingness of its audience to believe. As we can see, several cultural influences have culminated in recent years that have made this way of lying more effective and at the same time more irresistible.

TECHNICAL EXPERTISE HAS BOOSTED CREDIBILITY OF JUNK.

We have always relied on the quality of a given presentation to derive its credibility. The more sophisticated the technology, the more infrastructure, and the greater the polish used to disseminate the information, the more trustworthy it is thought to be. This is the principle behind the production of elaborate coins or bills to fight counterfeiting—the more embellished the money is, the harder it is to produce, and the harder it is to counterfeit. Check out the new one-hundred-dollar bill, and you'll see some pretty amazing security features employed for this very purpose.

News production has relied on this very principle. Regard the long-standing respect that the printed word demanded since the invention of the printing press; regard the kind of reverence the big three news stations commanded during the heyday of broadcast television. If you were in the position to create such content, you were bound to ensure that content was trustworthy, and so audiences could rely on high quality as a way to discriminate between real and fake news.

These days, the principle is rather flipped. Any schmoe can produce a newspaper or video broadcast, and he can do so with increasing quality. What's more, in the Internet Age, it's the tech-savvy young upstarts that are capable of creating the most powerful media, and the stodgy old behemoths that have failed to stay relevant. New media outlets such as Now This, AJ+, RT, The Blaze, and The Young Turks put out slick videos that bear all the marks of integrity that NBC, CBS, and ABC used to monopolize, but without a modicum of the traditional quality of fact checking and reporting that their predecessors offered.

The result is a clip such as this supposed report on the 2017 March for Life by RT (Russian Times):

The anchor looks and acts like a Walter Cronkite, and the video clip backdrop and glitzy ticker at the bottom scream integrity. But his words are little more than propaganda, and the opinionated argument he makes is not defended by any amount of logic.

With this and countless other sources, it is as though the counterfeit bills are more sophisticated than the legitimate ones. We no longer have the luxury of associating technical expertise with quality content; and so have lost a powerful tool in fighting off fake news.

Divisiveness Has Stretched Credulity.

Soon after the election, it was common to hear Democrats fretting over the fact that their candidate lost despite winning the popular vote (Clinton secured almost three million more votes nationwide). Not long after that, fringe agencies on the Right could be seen denying this data-driven fact with the claim that indeed Trump did win the popular vote despite what those on the Left were saying. At first, they relied on the logic that many of the counties' votes had not been tabulated yet and projected that, with the remaining votes, Trump would end up with more. Then, when that became impossible, they started cherry-picking the vote: Trump won in a landslide in the heartland (no kidding); Trump got more votes if you discount the illegal immigrant vote (claimed by the president himself); Trump won the popular vote if you exclude California (Calexit, anyone?). But these qualifications didn't make it into the narrative. By mid-December, *NY Magazine* reported that more than half of Republicans thought that Trump won the popular vote outright.

While some of these latter arguments might be based in truth, the notion that Trump won the popular vote cannot be defended. But that didn't stop media outlets from pumping their channels full of that misinformation. Nor did it stop consumers from gobbling it up.

One might be able to understand the rationale from the ardent Republican standpoint: If our candidate lost the popular vote, our victory wouldn't be fully legitimate. If our victory isn't legitimate, then we aren't vindicated. So, anything that contradicts the popular vote argument should be supported and shared no matter what bizarre logic is used in the process.

When times are divisive, people prioritize beating the other guy over truth and justice. The more divisive the times get, the greater the incentive to eschew truth and justice in order to win.

Coupled with the technical sorting algorithm of social media, the content that folks receive is fortified in what is called an 'echo chamber' and the incredulous becomes all the more credible. A fascinating study shows how two different Facebook users see the news in their feeds according to their supposed political affiliation.

Hyper Sociality Has Compelled Exaggeration.

In the pursuit of likes, producers of content are incentivized to put out the most outrageous and far-fetched stories. This has been an issue since the invention of communication sometime before the Internet. But, with the reach of social media, we have seen a greater potential impact and, as a result, a greater reward for 'going viral'. Folks have become overnight successes thanks to one video; fortunes can be made with the right message.

This is why we see people posting false information that seemingly has no real consequence. In 2012, a meme circulated that said that said some date in 2012, not the actual 2015, was the date that Marty went to in *Back to the Future II*. Why would anyone bother? The answer must be that they did it for instant clicks—it's an interesting thought (that we're living in a time when a popular movie was portrayed), and they couldn't wait until the real date. So they created a fake meme, called it 'Back to the Future Day', and it spread like wildfire.

I once saw a meme that said there was going to be a full moon on Friday the 13th one May, when, in reality, it was just going to be Friday the 13th (the moon was in crescent phase). Why would anyone blatantly lie about something so silly? The only answer is for clicks.

In a social age, only information that is controversial, sensational, and incredible makes the rounds. The more controversial, sensational, and incredible, the better. Savvy communicators realize this and adjust their stories to spark the greatest interest. We see it in everyday interaction as people get more of a response from an exaggerated story than one that just tells the facts. I was on a plane before a cross-country flight and someone thought it was a good idea to yell "Free Liberia!" It was nothing more than a stupid joke coming from someone who didn't realize the seriousness of his actions, but it forced the crew to deplane and all of the passengers to reroute. As they were facilitating, I heard someone calling his friend to explain he would be late. As he described the incident, he said that "Someone started screaming like a madman." Of course, his friend was thoroughly engaged with the story and wanted more. It didn't matter that that really didn't happen; what mattered is that he had an engaged audience.

In a social age, we are incentivized to exaggerate, embroider, embellish, overstate, distort, and heighten for effect if we hope to be heard at all. The best find ways to do so without stretching the truth, but most don't see the truth as a necessary restriction on a good performance. Speech coach James C. Humes even went so far as to encourage changing up facts of stories to personalize and make relevant. The idea is that there is a need for good, powerful communication, and, as long as the message is strong, details and facts can be overlooked.

Social media, with its tendency toward click-bait headlines and its users' aversion to actually reading the articles, exaggerate the exaggeration.

Imprecision Lends to Crying Wolf.

Careless exaggeration is seen clearly in the use and abuse of metaphors. Critics of a given group or behavior might compare that group or behavior to a well vilified subject to paint their target in a bad light. Critics of porn call it a form of abuse, for example, critics of state government call taxes theft, critics of Trump call him a Nazi.

Instead of worsening the image of their target, they tend only to blur the meaning of the invectives used, thus making metaphor less effective. If everyone you disagree with is Hitler, then your audience is numbed by the time a real Hitler does come by and start doing the bad things you fear.

Recently, feminists have called the effort to defund Planned Parenthood a form of assault on women. The argument is understandable for those who take access to abortion services personally, but the fact is that assault has a very technical and terrible connotation, which does not include taking away government funds. If we exaggerate the trauma of such an action, we don't make it worse in the eyes of our opponents, but rather make the real trauma less grievous. It is a form of the old Boy Who Cried Wolf saw—if everything is a wolf, even when it's not, then no one will believe you when the real wolf appears.

The extreme is seen in the use of the term 'hate speech' to arraign anyone who disagrees with us, and the simultaneous effort to make illegal any use of such speech. It is clear from the perspective of the bystander that it is an effort to silence dissent and ultimately control thought. By turning thought into action and turning action into criminal violence, exponents of hate speech wield a tremendous amount of influence. But, if thought is violence, then what recourse do we have for actual violent acts?

Famous Quotes Need Famous Mouths.

The saying "Famous quotes need famous mouths" is attributed to writer Ralph Keyes. It would probably be shared more if it were attributed Abraham Lincoln. The truth of the saying can be seen throughout the social media and even as high as presidential speeches, as almost everything worth sharing has been attributed to the great statesman.

It's true: Good ideas get far more reach when they are accompanied by a famous attribution. And so a message that needs to be heard, it is thought, needs to be attributed to a famous historical figure. What follows is a distorted view of history and usually a discrediting of what was really said.

We see it in the ridiculous Steve Jobs deathbed meme. The story is that Steve Jobs put together a little speech on his deathbed that renounced wealth and material things and praised love and treating others well. It's a nice thought, but he said nothing of the sort. First of all, Steve Jobs was never some money-grubbing capitalist. He was powerful at the head of Apple, but his salary was famously just $1. Secondly, he was so stubborn that it would be a stretch to believe that he would convert to anything, even on his deathbed. But this didn't stop people from spreading the falsehood. The message is positive and people want to spread positive messages. And, in order to do so, they attribute it to a famous if implausible speaker and the message takes off. I once saw the story posted by an executive at a Fortune 200 company.

You can't really say, "Wouldn't it be nice if Steve Jobs had said this" or "Steve Jobs might have said this". To make an impact, you have to make the direct attribution. Once you do, the message loses its credibility.

In 2016, a meme inspired by C.S. Lewis' *Screwtape Letters* made the rounds with a message of unity. Of course, the owner didn't say that it was inspired by *Screwtape*, she said that it came from the actual work. It is likely that she didn't mean to really attribute it to the legendary tale, but it would have been cumbersome to say that it was 'inspired by', so that was left out and the impression was that good ol' C.S. Lewis predicted our current age with the message.

Satire Is the New News.

In a scathing post-election report, comedian John Oliver of HBO's Last Week Tonight, blamed Trump's victory on what he called "fake facts".

Stringing up sites like Breitbart, Addicting Info, and Freedom Daily, Oliver showed how intentionally misleading news swayed opinion and how social media 'echo chambers' amplified the misinformation. What he forgot to point out is that he was part of the problem.

Oliver's show follows in a successful line of news parodies that began with Saturday Night Live's Weekend Update and continued with The Onion and then Comedy Central's Daily Show and Colbert Report. The original idea was to mock the otherwise staid news media with farcical reports and interviews. Thirty years ago, no one could have mistaken those parodies for real news since real news was more respected and the fake stuff was clearly satirical.

Now, it's not as clear cut. Traditional news media have lost credibility due to their inability to remain objective, and, meanwhile, the comedy shows appear more credible since they never had to be objective in the first place. One poll said that some 45% of self-identified liberals trusted what they saw on Jon Stewart's Daily Show. Obama has made appearances on both The Daily Show and Colbert Report. And, Stephen Colbert has testified in character before a congressional hearing.

Oliver takes it to the next level. He maintains that he is not a journalist, but the fact is that he does everything to persuade his audience that he is: He is seated at a news anchor desk, presents well-researched material on under-reported topics, and has a fancy city skyline as a backdrop. He claims that they fact check everything on the show as if to suggest that they are above the board of fake news, and yet every argument he makes is riddled with straw men fallacies, inconsistencies, and childish insults. He protects himself with the notion that he is not supposed to be news, and yet many still trust him as such and he uses that authority to spread specious logic far and wide.

This trend in satire reflects a broader trend in humor generally toward sarcasm. As Tom Wolfe chronicles in his 2004 *I Am Charlotte Simmons*, sarcasm is based in the amount of hurt that is levied on the butt of the joke. The more subtle the sarcasm is, the longer it takes to get, the more hurt that is inflicted. As such, the younger masters at sarcasm have even split the genre into three categories, 'Sarc One', 'Sarc Two', and 'Sarc Three'. Progressing from Sarc One to Three takes you from regular, fairly obvious sarcasm like "Cerise is such an in color this year" to nearly impossible to discern "I love that shirt. It'll be perfect for job interviews, and it'll be perfect for community service."

The best humor these days is nearly imperceptible from straightforward communication. The Simpsons' sharp commentary reflected this fact in a show titled 'Homerpalooza'. As Homer's character was making his way into view, one of the slacker youths in the audience said "Oh here comes that cannonball guy, he's cool." To which his friend asks, "Are you being sarcastic, dude?" And the first replies, "I don't even know anymore."

In the new century it is impossible to discern sarcasm from sincerity, and, as we've discovered, satire from journalism.

It has gotten to the point that satirical shows such as SNL's Weekend Update and John Oliver's Last Week Tonight have found it necessary to break away from their usually ambiguous humor to state cold facts so as to dissolve any potential confusion. When Seth Myers had a caricature of a crazed Republican on the show, he didn't answer her outlandish claim that Obama was a Muslim from Kenya with wit or even more jokes; he was obliged to say flatly, "No, he isn't." These days, comedy is the victim of its own success.

Relativism Reigns.

What is most ironic about this fake news foofaraw is that the ones who are most outraged by the fact that fake news might have swayed the election (like John Oliver and his followers) are the very ones who would subscribe to the philosophical principle of relativism. They subscribe to the most acclaimed philosophers, pundits, and intellectuals of the last hundred years who have said that all truth is relative and anyone purporting to assert universal truths is wrong and probably dangerous.

As Allan Bloom explained in his landmark *Closing of the American Mind*, our culture has equipped us with a framework of openness from early ages, such that no one has the right to assert anything absolutely. All must be accepted and all must be embraced as equally valuable.

We see it in Freud, who argued that all reason is just rationalizing our base instincts; we see it in Deconstructionism, which claims that words cannot possibly represent meaning; we see it in the multiculturalism which asserts that no given culture is morally superior to others; we see it in Behavioral Economics which states that we are all irrational and cannot help but to hinder our own best interests; we see it in modern parenting, which is defined by what might be called 'trophyism', or the eagerness for parents, teachers, and coaches to reward children when they haven't done anything notable; we see it most recently in the transgender fad in which everyone is encouraged to express him or herself anyway he or she likes even if it means transforming his or her himness or herness.

Relativism has been with us a while. It is the fruit of 13th century philosopher William of Ockham's Nominalism which states that there can be no universals, only specifics. Ockham was a serious philosopher, and his idea was highly controversial. The upshot was clear: If there are no universal truths, then whatever one wants to be true is true. The more people that believe a certain thing, the truer it becomes. Thus, those who are most vocal, most popular, and most forceful get to determine what the truth is for the populace. Ultimately, we are led to the stance that Thrasymachus takes in Plato's *Republic*: Might makes right; justice is power.

In *Hamlet*, Shakespeare has the prince offer up a bit of philosophy that summarizes the issue: "There is nothing good or bad, but thinking makes it so." It is the foundation of Positivism and ultimately Nihilism because the thought that nothing has meaning is necessarily contradictory and destroys itself. As Peter Kreeft explains, "The skeptic must say that it is true that there is no truth; or it is certain that there is no certainty; or it is objectively true that truth is not objective; or I know that I cannot know; or even it is only probable that there is only probability; or there are absolutely no absolutes; or it's a universal truth that no truth is universal."

As a culture, we have combated this tempting philosophy through right reason and a politico-economic system that protects freedom of thought. Throughout the 20th century, various forces have combined to break down our ability to fend off Nominalism to the extent that most live by the philosophy if not overtly champion it.

Now, with the technology of the Internet and our hyper sociality, the barriers to Nominalism have fallen completely, and we suddenly hear warning cries from all around: 'We have entered the Post-Truth Era—our culture is doomed!' The warning would be taken more seriously if it weren't being broadcast by those who so adamantly ushered us into this era.

In a classic parody, the *Onion*-esque religious satire site *The Babylon Bee* posted an ingenious article titled "Culture In Which All Truth Is Relative Suddenly Concerned About Fake News". In a swift blow, it summarized the utter hypocrisy of the whole movement: " 'It's just absolutely wrong, in my opinion,' said the man who doesn't believe in absolute ideals of right and wrong at all. 'What if someone reads the information and gets like, deceived? That just seems totally wicked.' "

It would be funny if it weren't absolutely true.

—January 2017

LOGIC IN THE TIME OF CORONA

THE FIRST CASUALTY IN THE Coronavirus Pandemic was reason. Even before the WHO Issued its first warnings, experts were jumping to conclusions and average people were spouting fallacies like sophists at a feast. The main driver was fear, and, in times of great stress, fear begets panic, and panic begets madness. As it turns out, delusion is more contagious than the virus. What might have been a routine emergency response turned into an unprecedented disaster, the scope of which we have not yet begun to realize.

There are those who will argue that we can never know whether a universal lockdown was an overreaction. Even if Coronavirus causes as many deaths as a severe flu season, people will say that it would have been an order of magnitude worse if we had done nothing. But a simple thought experiment proves that we've gone too far: If Coronavirus is as dangerous as they said, then we can't lift the lockdown until we have achieved herd immunity. But we can't achieve herd immunity until we lift the lockdown. Some have begun to see this Catch-22, and have called for a calculated reopening, which may prove to be the only viable way out.

Meanwhile, it will be constructive to review our major miscues leading up to this conundrum with the hope that next time we might avoid such catastrophic decision-making. Here, then, is a short history of Coronavirus in logical fallacies.

"If we don't do anything, 40 million could die."

The spark that ignited the panic is doubtless a report published by a team of researchers at Imperial College London, which warned that COVID-19 could infect up to 7 billion people worldwide and cause some 40 million deaths. With such alarming figures, government officials everywhere started shutting down businesses and enforcing large-scale 'social distancing' measures. But the paper was based on early and incomplete data, and it was not peer reviewed. Now that we've gained more knowledge on the disease, the Imperial College team has revised their models. But it was too late; decisions had been made that would alter the course of history.

Fallacy: Jumping to Conclusions.

"People are dying!"

Not long after the lockdowns started up, a story began to circulate about a young woman who died waiting for a Coronavirus test. The implication was clear: Coronavirus wasn't just attacking the elderly or those who were immune-compromised as early reports had indicated. This thing could get anyone and kill in a quick, dramatic fashion. No one was safe, and we should all cower in closets in fear for the coming malady. As it turned out, the woman hadn't tested positive for Coronavirus after all. The hysteria was caused based on a strong belief by her boyfriend. Nonetheless, fear was spread. This kind of hysteria, multiplied manifold the last month or so has led to panic, which leads to several problems, including hoarding of survival supplies like masks, disinfectant, and, notoriously toilet paper, unnecessarily draining care facilities of needed goods, and putting undue strain on the system. It also prompts people to rush to the hospital when they think they might have the disease (even when they don't) and not go to the hospital when they need to go (as in the case of a patient with a heart condition or cancer) for fear of catching the thing.

Fallacies: Appeal to Fear, Appeal to Emotion.

"If you're not an epidemiologist or doctor, you don't have a say."

Very early on in this debacle, it became clear that the only people we could listen to were experts—epidemiologists, health care professionals, and, of course, Bill Gates. Everyone else would have to keep quiet and do as we were told. Economists, statisticians, politicians, ethicists, business owners, part-time workers, teachers, theologians—all might have valuable input into how we respond to this thing, but, no matter since these folks don't have the right credentials. Oh, you have a well-thought-out essay on the plight of the 30 million unemployed caused by the lockdown? I won't listen because it's not by an epidemiologist! And then there's YouTube's banning anything that goes against the WHO. Of course, YouTube is a veteran at logical fallacies.

Fallacies: Appeal to Authority, Genetic Fallacy.

"You don't want to see 10% of Americans dying, do you?"

I once read a post from a doctor which said something to the effect of "Italy has reported a 10% death rate. You don't want to see 10% of Americans dying, do you?" There are so many things wrong with this, it gave me vertigo. First, the 10% death rate in Italy was based on known cases, which isn't how epidemiologists measure death rate. The typical approach is to base it on infections, which isn't known now and can only be estimated later. As we discover more, we find that infections are much higher than previously thought to be, and the vast majority of infections are asymptomatic, which means that the actual death rate is much lower than expected. One study found it to be around 0.1-0.2%, which happens to be around the same rate as the flu. But this doctor wasn't done. He went on to suggest that the 10% death rate would mean that 10% of an entire population would die because of the disease. No amount of backtracking can correct this atrocious thought process.

Fallacy: Conflation.

"The disease spreads through close social contact with infected persons, so we need to eliminate all social contact."

On a basic level, the concept of social distancing makes a lot of sense. My inner introvert would say that we should have been practicing this as a matter of course. But it doesn't take an extreme extrovert to see the fallacy in the draconian rules laid down by government officials. Yes, the disease is spread through social contact, but that doesn't mean that all social contact spreads the disease. If you're sick or if you're vulnerable, don't come into contact with others. It might be that simple.

Fallacy: Part to Whole.

"You want to open the economy? You must want people to die."

To many, this situation is simple: the Coronavirus threat is so great that complete lockdown is the only way we can avoid the loss of millions. To these, anyone who would open the economy must not only be okay with the death of millions, but must positively desire it. Of course, to any open-eyed observer, there are alternative views. It is possible that many will die despite a lockdown. And, as Sweden and Japan have shown, it is possible that opening the economy will not cause many more deaths in the short term, and might prevent deaths in the long term.

Fallacy: False Dichotomy.

"The curve is flattening—the lockdown is working!"

All signs indicate that countries who have instituted lockdowns and stay-at-home orders have successfully begun to flatten the curve. But it is a fallacy to conclude that the flattening was due to the lockdowns themselves.

As some countries have demonstrated, it was possible to flatten the curve even without shutting down the economy. Others have argued that the disease would have spread in a predictable pattern no matter what we did. It is reasonable to conclude that the lockdowns did lead to more social distancing and that social distancing led to a lower rate of transmission. But can it be said that the lockdown was what did the trick? In an episode of The Simpsons, Homer delights in the false sense of security: "Not a bear in sight—The Bear Patrol must be working!" Then Lisa schools him on logical fallacies. Don't let's be Homer.

Fallacies: Post Hoc Ergo Propter Hoc, Affirming the Consequent.

"THE CORONAVIRUS PANDEMIC WILL CAUSE FAMINES OF BIBLICAL PROPORTIONS."

Everyone is coming to grips with the fact that the economy is going through a catastrophic contraction the likes of which we haven't seen since the days of The Old Testament. Thirty million unemployed in five weeks, hotels and restaurants closing their doors, companies fearing default, trillions of dollars of stimulus money being churned out to prevent collapse and the perverse economic distortion that has come from it, and supply chains grinding to a halt. But it must be recognized that none of this was due to the virus itself. All of it was due to our reaction to the virus, policy that has forced this calamity on the world. Blaming the virus reassures us that we did all we could to stop an existential threat. But the honest observer will realize that the destruction caused by the virus pales in comparison to the damage done by knee-jerk hypochondriacs and opportunistic totalitarians.

Fallacy: False Cause.

* * *

It's hard to identify the post-apocalyptic tale that best foreshadows this life in the time of Corona. But, if there is one that reliably gets our time right, it would be The Twilight Zone. In an episode titled "The Shelter", we see what happens when a community encounters an existential crisis similar to that of our own. A government official announces over the radio that they have detected nuclear missiles headed for New York and commands everyone take shelter. Panic comes over the families who have not built their own shelters, and soon they degrade into savages to break into the lone shelter on the block.

Though the threat is of a different nature, the situation is the same. Watching the short 30-minute show is a bit like looking into a sociological mirror: Fear leads to panic, which leads to madness. All common sense and mores are abandoned in the bitter struggle to survive.

At the end of the episode, we hear the official announce that they have identified the objects as satellites—there was no nuclear threat after all, and everyone can go back to life as normal. Ashamed, everyone apologizes. And yet, the drill has revealed just how frail that normal life had been and just how quickly everyone had given up the common sense that sustained it.

—April 2020

THE DEATH
OF DISSENT

IN THE AFTERMATH OF THE horrific attack in Orlando, we have witnessed a death that is equally troubling if only because of its scope and the fact that no one is talking about it—the death of dissent.

Sympathy and support for the mostly gay victims has come from all corners of society including charitable gestures from Christians, Muslims, and others who are considered anti-gay. The sympathy and support is not what's troubling. What's troubling is that the sympathy and support have been rejected.

Anderson Cooper famously grilled Florida Attorney General, who has previously fought against same-sex marriage, suggesting that someone who is opposed to same-sex marriage would be hypocritical to support the victims of the Orlando crime. The mayor of San Antonio was shamed at a vigil for being "part of the hurt". Across social media, the folks in the LGBT community have challenged Christians who show compassion for gays after Orlando when they for so long fought against them. Some went so far as to condemn Christianity as the cause of the Orlando massacre.

Christians who offered support for the Orlando victims were practicing the traditional Christ-like policy of 'love the sinner, hate the sin'. They forgot that many have identified themselves by their sin, and so hating the sin means hating them as individuals. They don't believe they are sinners, and so don't need their compassion anyway.

This kind of all-or-nothing mentality has rather defined the LGBT movement for quite a while now, and can be seen in full force in this latest episode. On social media, in politics, and at the workplace, sympathy for the Orlando shooting victims has seamlessly morphed into solidarity with the gay community. The symbol of support was not the Orlando or Florida flag but the multicolored 'gay flag', and could be seen on the Facebook temporary profile pictures, memorial lights, and armbands.

And, while it makes perfect sense for those who want to show sympathy for the victims to also show their solidarity with the LGBT community, it has become a requisite, and anyone who doesn't show solidarity with the LGBT community is censured.

One vocal progressive at my office took the opportunity to post a message which encouraged everyone to actively speak out in defense of the LGBT community and to not accept dehumanizing attitudes, speech, or actions they come across. It could easily be inferred that anyone who does not actively speak out in defense of the LGBT community must be part of the dehumanizing effort that culminated in the Orlando shooting.

The message being sent is clear: 'You are with us or you're against us. If you want to support the victims of the shooting, then you must also support everything they stood for. If you don't support the LGBT community and everything they stand for, then you're a perpetrator of hate, just like the terrorist in Orlando, and most likely no better.'

The objective bystander might wonder whether we're missing a key perspective here. Can't we mourn for the victims of the Orlando shooting, not as gay people, but simply as people? Can't we support them as Americans, as free persons who can choose their lifestyle, and still not support their lifestyle? Can't we deplore the actions of the terrorist and still disagree with the actions of the victims?

Just because the terrorist was wrong doesn't mean the victims and their community should have license to do whatever they want. Just because we face one evil doesn't mean we should accept all others.

In the aftermath of the tragedy, the outpouring of sympathy immediately turned into a list of demands—all should show their support for the LGBT community or else be branded a hater and linked with the terrorist in mentality if not in action. As it was in the response of other politically-charged shootings (i.e., Charleston), and not unlike the response after 9/11, the prevailing milieu is that you're either with us or against us, and if you're against us, then you're with the enemy, you are the enemy.

This is the standard in the modern hyper-social and childishly liberal age: If you're against Obama, you're racist; if you're against Hillary, you're sexist; if you're against same-sex marriage, you're homophobic; if you're against so-called 'radical Islam', you're Islamophobic. Basically, you can't be against anything without being a bigot, extremist, and reactionary. That is, unless you're against gun rights, the Constitution, and Republicans.

And this is the problem: If you oppose the prevailing standard, if you sail against the wind, then you will be labeled 'apostate' and banished from our society. Democratic tyranny it may be—tyranny of the majority—but it is tyranny nonetheless.

Now, America is no stranger to the tyranny of the majority. We have seen it since the days of Tocqueville and the age of the Internet has only intensified the issue. It has come to a point where this tyranny is leading to outright censorship (i.e., Facebook) and legal and criminal repercussions (i.e., IRS). In California, it will soon be illegal to question Global Warming. The concept of Hate Crime has already had a chilling effect on the way people talk.

> The sovereign can no longer say, "You shall think as I do on the pain of death;" but he says, "You are free to think differently from me, and to retain your life, your property, and all that you possess; but if such be our determination, you are henceforth an alien among your people. You may retain your civil rights, but they will be useless to you, for you will never be chosen by your fellow-citizens if you solicit their suffrages, and they will affect to scorn you if you solicit their esteem. You will remain among men, but you will be deprived of the rights of mankind. Your fellow-creatures will shun you like an impure being, and those who are most persuaded of your innocence will abandon you too, lest they should be shunned in their turn. Go in peace! I have given you your life, but it is an existence incomparably worse than death.

—Alexis de Tocqueville, *Democracy in America* (1835)

Even though America is familiar with the tyranny of the majority, it has always offered recourse in the form of dissent. The Declaration of Independence is one huge statement of dissent, and in it and the Constitution is a guarantee of dissent. It could be argued that America, as a Democratic Republic, with elections seemingly every year, is a form of perpetual dissent. The ability to disagree and move on to something that you want is at the very core of this country, and has in many ways enabled the great growth and production and innovation that we have always been known for.

But we have forgotten that dissent does not have to lead to hatred, and hatred does not have to lead to violence. These days, we have identified ourselves as the sins we commit, and built up a great infrastructure of incentives and tax breaks to bolster those identities. As such, anyone who disagrees with our sins invariably disagrees with us as human beings. We have lost the ability to peaceably disagree.

And isn't that a sad state of affairs? If we are no longer able to dissent and live our lives as individuals apart from the tyranny of the majority, if we can no longer disagree with the way people live their lives and still peaceably live beside them, then we have lost what it is to be American, and we are ultimately no better than the terrorists whose only way of dissent is through violence.

This is the irony of our intolerant tolerance. Folks like Anderson Cooper and the vocal supporters of the LGBT community might mean well by imposing their beliefs on others, but, by forcing dissenters to agree with them, it is they who are like the Orlando terrorist, not the dissenters. The only way they can succeed in achieving the rights they seek is to live in a world where we can agree to disagree. And that means being humble, and accepting the sympathy from those who disagree with their lifestyle. Please allow Christians to mourn the Orlando victims. And please allow them to disagree with their lifestyle at the same time. Unless we do, all that is American is lost.

—June 2016

HOW WE GOT RIGHTS SO WRONG

IF THE RECENT DEBATE OVER RFRA laws and same-sex marriage teaches us anything, it is not that there are a bunch of bigots out there or that there are people being unjustly discriminated against. It is that, as a nation, we are facing a crisis of rights.

Witness the recent news item from Oregon: Last month, a judge pronounced that two bakers should pay $135,000 in damages for refusing to bake a same-sex wedding cake.

Now, we can look at this from a few angles. It could be that a couple of bigots are getting what they deserve. Or it could be that they are being unfairly demonized for doing their conscience. There are good people with good arguments on both sides of the debate.

We can all agree, however, that the Oregon case signifies a clash between opposing rights. Both sides of the argument claim to be in the right and to have the right to do what they are doing. On the one side are the bakers' rights to conduct business as they please and to practice their conscience. On the other side are the customers' rights to buy available goods and to not be discriminated against. The bakers' rights necessarily infringe upon the customers' rights, and vice versa.

One is tempted to chalk up the skirmish to an inevitable consequence of rights. The thought is that people want different things, and sometimes those wants come into conflict with each other. As it is with a rancher who wants to herd his cattle on someone else's pasture, or the driver who wants to cut someone off while exiting the highway, sometimes it's just 'my rights versus yours'.

But, more than anything, this underscores a deep misunderstanding of the concept of rights. It is to assume that all rights are the same, and all conflict between them is an inner conflict within a self-contradictory system. We blithely accept the idea that the bakers' rights are the same as the customers' rights because, of course, they are both called 'rights'.

A closer look reveals that the rights concerned are substantively different even though they use the same appellation. The fact is that the bakers' rights do not force anyone to do anything while the customers' rights more or less force the bakers to do something, and particularly something that would go against their consciences. This discrepancy means everything, and highlights the difference between two conflicting, even contradictory sets of rights.

ALL RIGHTS ARE NOT CREATED EQUAL.

We can turn to the work of Czech-French jurist Karel Vašák for elucidation. Vašák outlined what he called 'three generations of rights', which take us from the origins of the concept of rights in the 17th and 18th centuries to the present day. They follow in order the three themes of the French Revolutionary apothegm, 'Liberté, Equalité, Fraternité'.

The first generation of rights, Liberté, consists in what might be called Natural Rights or the Rights of Man. Conceived as early as Aquinas and enumerated by Locke, Montesquieu, and the Founders of the United States of America, these rights were seen largely as universal, God-given rights that no other citizen or government could add or take away. Hence the descriptor 'natural'—they apply to all men for the very sake that makes them men, access to God's law through right reason.

Due to these qualities, there are relatively few such rights. Locke summed them up as three: Life, Liberty, and Property. These three were acknowledged through the Declaration of Independence and American Revolution. The Bill of Rights provided specific examples such as freedom of speech, freedom to bear arms, and the right to a fair trial, but the core principle was the same.

From the Founding, Natural Rights stood for more than a century as the basis for all new socio-political constructs. Shortly after the turn of the 20th century, however, we began to see an indication that Natural Rights are not sufficient to provide the greatest well-being possible. Even though there was freedom and opportunity, there was also widespread indigence, hardship, and suffering.

And so, in the first half of the 20th century, thinkers and politicians sought to introduce another wave of rights, Vašák's second generation, or Equalité rights. This second wave took what had begun as Welfare State arrangements and turned them into entitlements—clean and safe jobs, food, housing, education, healthcare, and old-age pensions. This is where we get Franklin Roosevelt's Second Bill of Rights, a smorgasbord that even included leisure as an entitlement.

The third generation of rights, Fraternité, departed even further from the origin of Natural Rights. The idea was that, to live a fulfilled life, one must have, not only life and liberty, and not only food and shelter, but also less tangible and at the same time more costly conditions and opportunities. Enumerated in post-modern, international documents such as the 1972 Stockholm Declaration and the 1992 Rio Declaration, the third generation includes group rights, such as those that recognize and support indigenous peoples, ethnic minorities, women, children, disabled persons, and so-called 'protected classes'; the right to self-determination; the right to a healthy environment; and the right to take part in a cultural heritage. This third generation is where anti-discrimination rights reside.

Not all of the rights from any of the generations have been directly codified into law. But the concepts permeate the culture and animate activists to the extent that the spirit of each is broadly reflected into legislation or court decisions. And so it can be said that each generation of rights is backed by force as well as cultural inertia.

The second and third generation rights, or what have been called 'Civil Rights', are sometimes said to be an extension of Natural Rights in that they add to the Natural Rights of life and liberty as the Bill of Rights did. But all would recognize there are critical differences. To begin, these new rights are not necessarily God-given. No one argues that the right to housing or cultural heritage is inalienable. It is understood that the state is necessary to bring them about, whence 'civil' (i.e., 'created by the civil authority') as opposed to 'natural'.

Nor are the second and third generation of rights universal. The bizarre Orwellian concept of 'protected classes' alone proves that these alleged rights are aimed not at all human beings for the sake that they are human beings, but rather for certain groups for the sake that they are different. While Natural Rights apply to and stress the similarities between people and thus unite, Civil Rights apply to and stress the differences between people and thus separate.

By the same token, whereas the first generation provides benefits of freedom without cost, the second and third provide benefits with a price tag. As political science professor Charles Kesler put it, creating rights creates duties to fulfill these rights. "As government grows, as more and more rights are created, someone has got to pay to guarantee your healthcare, your home, your job, your vacation from the job, and so forth." To provide the second and third generations of rights, government must pay for them, which means that it must obtain the revenue somehow, which means it must force the people to pay taxes or support regulations one way or another.

To provide vacations for everyone, the government must forcibly take money from taxpayers and give it to the vacationers; to ensure that same-sex couples are not discriminated against, the government must forcibly make bakers provide their wedding cake.

WHEN EVERYTHING IS A RIGHT, NOTHING IS A RIGHT.

Though proponents assert that all three generations of rights depend upon each other, it is clear that there is incongruity between the first and the other two generations. The difference can be seen in the proliferation of rights that we have seen in the last few decades. With Natural Rights, we could count on three fundamental entitlements; under the aegis of second and third generation rights, everything imaginable has become a right. Someone wants something and sees other people getting it, and so it must be a right. After all, why should someone else have something that all cannot have? Other people have high-paying jobs, so why cannot we? Other people have health insurance, so why cannot we? Other people are getting married, so why cannot we?

This is what the plausible concept of equal opportunity has morphed into: If some can have it, so must we all. It describes not a right, but a childish daydream. It is the elementary school concept of fairness writ large: 'Did little Johnny bring enough to share?' And, like all childish daydreams, it has no place in adult public affairs.

Indeed, labeling it a 'right' is not a matter of objective epistemology at all, but rather a deft stroke of political handiwork. By appropriating the label, opponents of rights have fortified their cause behind their enemy's city wall. To contradict something called 'gay rights' is to contradict the historical tradition of rights in general, and so no one ever dares.

Worst of all, the rise of the second and third generations of rights has destroyed the first. In order to grant minority rights, workers rights, and the like, state governments must force the people to provide the wanted goods and services. In order to provide high-paying jobs, government must force employers to pay their employees more; in order to provide health care, government must force hospitals to offer services they would otherwise deny; in order to protect against discrimination, government must force pastors and cake bakers to take part in disagreeable ceremonies. While it benefits the employees, patients, and marrying couples, it crushes the Natural Rights of the employers, medical practitioners, priests, and bakers. It would seem that we have forgotten the fact that a fundamental part of being able to do as one pleases is being able to not do what someone else pleases.

As Bastiat put it in response to Lamartine's plea for Fraternité, "The second half of your program will destroy the first half. It is quite impossible for me to conceive of fraternity as legally enforced, without liberty being legally destroyed, and justice being trampled underfoot."

Increasingly, as seen in the Oregon case, the courts are joining the legislatures in this rampage. This means that the courts are either redefining Liberté rights to include Equalité and Fraternité, or we are simply getting rid of Liberté altogether. The result of the late proliferation of rights, then, is the destruction of rights.

Critics will cry 'Hyperbole!' After all, it's just a cake—who cares if a baker is forced to bake a cake for someone? They're doing it anyway.

This is to miss the forest for the trees. The bakers say that the fine would ruin them financially. If they don't pay the fine, they will be sent to jail; if they refuse to go to jail, they will be forced; if they resist, they will be killed. Basically, the Oregon case means that we, as a society, are willing to kill someone for not baking a cake.

It might seem extreme, but that is exactly the proposition we face. Yale Law professor Stephen L. Carter explains that a law can only be viable if police are willing to enforce it, and the ultimate form of enforcement is through lethal violence. It is the explanation for the Eric Garner case and similar tragic stories that we've heard lately.

At the founding, political thinkers and lay citizens alike sought to establish a nation based on Natural Rights. The idea was that all had the right to do as they pleased so long as they didn't harm others' rights to do the same. Rights were supreme, and everyone could belong as long as they adhered to the basic principle of Natural Rights.

These days, as we have found, belonging is supreme, and you are only granted rights as long as you accept everyone and everything. Few have come to realize in this age of inclusiveness that accepting everyone and everything means that there can be no judgment, that without judgment there can be no discretion, without discretion there can be no choice, without choice there is no freedom, and without freedom rights are meaningless.

TWO RIGHTS MAKING A WRONG.

The progressive is compelled to protest. Isn't there at least some virtue in the second and third generations of rights? Life wasn't perfect when we were limited to Natural Rights, and so Civil Rights were necessary to fulfill the promise.

Consider slavery and the Jim Crow South. In America, for 150 years, we had an establishment of Natural Rights, and still the worst evil persisted. The argument goes, this evil could only be overcome by a new set of protections, even if those new protections undid some old ones.

But this is to suggest that the first generation of rights accommodated evils like slavery and Jim Crow laws. Of course, the right to Life, Liberty, and Property, granted to everyone by God explicitly condemns slavery and

Jim Crow laws, which could only exist in spite of Natural Rights. Regard the arguments made by abolitionists in the time of slavery and by integrationists in the time of Jim Crow: Reformers relied upon Natural Rights and the Founding documents for their case. That is because they understood that slavery and Jim Crow laws were violations of the fundamental Rights of Man, and all they had to do was to appeal to the people's sense of Natural Rights to convince.

Contrast that with the arguments used to overcome today's evils, discrimination, lack of vacation, and so on. Not only do today's activists not rely upon the Founding documents and Natural Rights to make their cases, they rather hold the Founders in contempt. They were racist aristocrats aimed at squirearchy, and so everything they stood for must be rejected.

This is to throw out the baby and keep the bathwater. The problem wasn't that Natural Rights allowed for evils to exist; it was that people in power codified evil despite Natural Rights. With Jim Crow, for example, the problem wasn't that people had the liberty to do as they pleased and used that liberty to discriminate; the problem was that governments and laws positively forced people to discriminate.

The solution, then, is not to correct or to get rid of Natural Rights in favor of Civil Rights; it is to correct or get rid of the laws that contradict Natural Rights. There is no need for new rights as long as the fundamental rights are enforced as designed.

And that is the trouble with Civil Rights or any of the second or third generation rights—what is good in them is redundant and thus useless; the rest defeats Natural Rights and is thus detrimental.

This is mirrored remarkably in the same-sex marriage conundrum. The problem isn't that people have the freedom to do as they please and use that freedom to discriminate; the problem is that governments and laws positively force people to discriminate.

Beyond the traditional meaning and customary sacrament that goes with marriage, it also comes with a number of civic privileges, including tax breaks, estate planning, employment, housing, and death benefits. The upshot is that people who are not married are necessarily discriminated against and denied these benefits. Government incents marriage and discriminates against non-married persons, so it only makes sense that people want to get married even if they cannot possibly fit into the category as traditionally defined.

The solution is not to redefine marriage so that others get the benefits; it is, rather to get rid of the benefits that married couples receive and that non-married persons are denied. The solution is to quit incenting marriage and legally discriminating against non-married persons. No new laws are needed to protect gay rights; Natural Rights should do the trick for all humans inasmuch as they define themselves as humans.

THE ONLY RIGHTS WE'RE LEFT WITH.

No one will deny that this is a complex and likely contentious solution. In a century of piling up rights, there are many who have derived valuable and even time-honored benefits. The point is not to punish those people from receiving those special benefits, but rather to ensure that all people receive the fundamental benefits of being alive. Indeed, getting rid of all the special rights and benefits is the only way we can protect the fundamental rights and benefits for all. For, as Jefferson said, "The most sacred of the duties of a government [is] to do equal and impartial justice to all its citizens." The only way to do that is to limit rights to the natural ones.

Wedding cake is not a right, just as same-sex marriage is not a right, just as marriage in general is not a right. There is no such thing as 'gay rights' or 'black rights' or 'reproductive rights' or 'student rights'. There are only 'Human Rights'. Advocates of gay marriage seek respect for being gay. But the Constitution doesn't guarantee respect for being gay or being straight or being white or being black. It guarantees respect for all humans as human beings, and makes no exceptions based on the distinctions we choose to emphasize.

This standard is the only viable standard for rights, and is so par excellence since it by nature exalts what is universal and highest in men—the ability to reason. Civil Rights divide and exalt the basest of man's characteristics—skin color, disabilities, sexual instincts. Contemporary political standards reduce men to these base characteristics. Only when we elevate our self-perception can rights grant us the dignity they promise.

From the 1966 film adaptation of *A Man for All Seasons*, a standard to perfect our nation: "I do none harm. I say none harm. I think none harm. And if this be not enough to keep a man alive, then in good faith, I long not to live."

—May 2015

THE
FIST

WHY ANTI-TRUMPERS MIGHT BE THE BIGGER PROBLEM

As 2016 Super Tuesday results filed in, a sinking feeling could be felt across the country. Political pundits and lay voters alike realized that Donald J. Trump had a good chance of securing a majority of the states' primaries, which meant that he could win Super Tuesday, and winning Super Tuesday could propel him toward the nomination, and if he won the nomination he could foreseeably win the presidency. That sinking feeling led to an eerie realization: The Donald could become president of the United States of America.

What had been an impossibility suddenly became real; what was for so long a joke was suddenly no laughing matter.

A chorus arose from the commentators, soft at first, but by Super Tuesday a full-blown bellow: Stop Trump! The Donald would be atrocious for American democracy, and we must do everything we can to prevent his nomination. People pulled out the stops; comparisons to Hitler were rife; Whoopi Goldberg threatened to leave America.

But, in reading over the commentary, hit pieces, and outright propaganda that arose to stop the unconventional candidate, it occurred to me that Trump really isn't the worst thing for American democracy—the troop of anti-Trumpers and their logic are. Sure, Trump is a clown and has no business being the president of the country. But the anti-Trump haters are out-clowning him, and almost making a Trump presidency appealing because of it.

Here's why:

TRUMP IS NO HITLER, AND CALLING HIM THAT SHOWS YOUR IGNORANCE.

In an interview with CNN, former Mexican president Vicente Fox said that Trump would take the U.S. back to the days of conflict, and that he reminded him of Hitler, quite as if he was around in the 1930s. This is not some random reflection; it's the norm. Pretty much everyone opposed to Trump compares him to Hitler. Cracked.com ran an article showing parallels between the rise of Trump and Hitler; The Huffington Post regularly compares Trump to Hitler; and even The Washington Post published an editorial in which the writer likened Trump's rise to that of Hitler.

It's not without reason. As a popular meme suggests, the similarities are striking, especially in their populism: Both Hitler and Trump rose to power as demagogic opportunists, vilifying a group of immigrants and exploiting a divided nation.

Okay, true, there is that connection. But, then again, pretty much all successful politicians these days can be said to have taken the same path— Hillary, Bernie, Obama, George W.—basically, the only way to rise to the top in today's political system is to be a demagogic opportunist exploiting a divided nation. You don't hear about politicians who aren't demagogic opportunists because they don't succeed. Rand Paul is an example of a politician who couldn't be considered a demagogic opportunist, same with Scott Walker, and Ben Carson, and any number of others who fell out of the race early. Someone else who is a demagogic opportunist always beats them and takes the crown.

It doesn't take much to see that the differences between Trump and Hitler far outweigh the similarities. Trump says some silly, vulgar, and often immoral things. But in no way has he ever advocated complete political upheaval, world domination, or genocide. He never would nor could—his supporters don't want that despite what the folks at HuffPo say.

Trump-haters draw conclusions about his statements and actions, but they are always something of a stretch and usually he equivocates and makes the statement more amenable after all—he did so with his ban on Muslim travel to the United States. He has to equivocate on anything that borders on authoritarianism because he knows his supporters don't want that and he doesn't want that.

Argumentum ad Hitlerum is a logical fallacy for a reason. It bypasses rigor and can lead down a dangerous path. John Oliver hinted at the extreme when he suggested that time travelers will come back to this point in history to "try and stop the whole thing". It's the implication of statements like that which make the anti-Trumpers more ridiculous—more dangerous—than Trump, himself.

While no one should justify Trump's demagoguery, it doesn't help to exaggerate it either. At the very least, it would do the anti-Trump crowd well to recognize the fact that not all demagogues are Hitler. I can tell you the story of a leader who rose to power on the strength of a controversial race-based proposal by exploiting a divided country, after which he violated his country's constitution, defied balances of power, prosecuted the deadliest war in his country's history, and was hated by half of his nation's population. That's not Hitler. That's Abraham Lincoln, someone whose greatness is hardly challenged by the anti-Trump group.

The problem isn't Trump, it's the system, and you don't fix the system by trashing Trump.

In his effort to stop "the most dangerous major presidential candidate in memory", Vox editor Ezra Klein said something very revealing. He said that being president is important because the president decides "which regulations to enforce and which to let go of."

Of course, living almost eight years under Obama and eight under George W. Bush, it might seem as though the president is in charge of deciding which rules to enforce, or even what rules there should be, because that's exactly what the system has become. If there's a program that the president wants, he'll ram it through until it's law; if there's a part of the law that he doesn't like, he won't enforce it.

The fact is that the executive office is not designed as a branch that writes the law and instead is a branch that enforces the laws that Congress writes. In our time, this fact goes unnoticed, as astutely pointed out by the jesters at Saturday Night Live.

The response is to be expected. If you think that the law of the land comes from the president, then it makes sense that you would do everything in your power to prevent Trump from getting to the White House. And yet you would be perpetuating a broken system. Keeping Trump out of the White House won't solve the problem because that's not the problem—the president dictating the law is the problem. Under such a broken system, any demagogue could come in and abuse power just as Obama is doing today. And that's the real problem.

More than anything, this underscores a powerful misunderstanding the anti-Trump crowd holds: Really, the problem is not Trump but rather the system that made Trump possible. And anyone who wants to fix it should focus attention on the system, not on Trump.

This goes for the two most audacious stances Trump has taken, that on Mexican illegal immigration and that on the Muslim refugee crisis. Trump-haters complain about his views on Mexican immigration and his moratorium on Muslim refugees, and conclude that he must be the problem—because he's so mean. But Trump is simply responding to a problem in the system. True, his proposed solutions are callous and rather asinine, but to focus on his proposals is to miss the point that we've got a jacked up system, and that's what needs to be fixed.

To begin to solve the problems in the immigration and refugee systems, we'd have to sincerely look at the causes of those problems. For example, no one will doubt that we have an immigration problem. To truly consider fixing it, we'd have to look at our immigration policies, and the incentives pushing migrants north such as the drug war and our generous welfare system. Similarly, no one will doubt that the Middle Eastern refugee crisis is a major problem. To truly consider fixing it, we'd have to look at our foreign policy and that of the U.N. relocation system. We cannot fix the problems unless we get at the root.

It is easy for anti-Trumpers to view these issues from a purely compassionate perspective. The most compassionate here want to accept everyone into our country, place them in comfortable homes, and give them free university education. Of course, Trump sees such compassion from a business standpoint. And, from a business standpoint, as he has put it, we're getting ripped off. Simply, the way the system works, we are in no way capable of accommodating such an influx. The welfare system has been stretched beyond functionality for some time, the debt is skyrocketing, and reform is not within sight. But without reforming our welfare and economic policies, the compassionate intake of any and all will be economically disastrous.

Trump sees this. What he is insisting on (however inarticulately) is the fact that the system is broken. Haters would be more helpful if, instead of trashing Trump's silly proposals, they actually proposed solutions that took into account the very important considerations that drive Trump's proposals. That's harder than one might assume.

Ultimately, you can't seriously consider opening borders without talking welfare reform and scaling back the drug war; you can't seriously welcome all refugees without talking about reforming the U.N. refugee policy and scaling back our nation-building efforts. Perhaps the haters should refocus their energy on real solutions as opposed to just trashing The Donald.

IF YOU'RE GOING TO CRITICIZE TRUMP FOR BEING UNDEMOCRATIC, YOU PROBABLY SHOULDN'T BE UNDEMOCRATIC YOURSELF.

In a *Washington Post* editorial, author Danielle Allen claims that it has become a matter of existential urgency to stop Trump before the general election. The reason, of course, is that Trump would destroy American democracy, so we need to prevent him from getting closer to the presidency. The problem is that the author's proposal on how to stop him is awfully anti-American and undemocratic itself.

First of all, she's a Democrat voting for Hillary, so her attempt to sway the Republican primary is disingenuous. It's like the Slate writer lamenting about how Trump is destroying the GOP and what they need to do to rebuild. The only interest that Slate has in the GOP is as a whipping boy. They don't want to see it go away, but it's not in the interest of the GOP that it sticks around. Perhaps Ms. Allen wants Trump to go away, but it might be more self-serving than she lets on.

Second, the methods she proposes border on Trump-esque tactics. Journalists should not cover the Trump campaign to effectively censure him; Democrats should re-register and vote for Rubio; Republicans should renounce their support for Trump. These are suspicious measures for someone whose favorite candidate looks to face Trump in what will be an "unpredictable" general election. Certainly, these measures defy the democratic process, which, more or less undermines her whole argument.

This is only the start. We hear of protesters sucker punching Trump supporters, slinging insults, and, calls for assassination. As Dilbert creator Scott Adams put it, "The media, the public, and the other candidates are creating a situation that is deeply dangerous for Trump. I put the odds of an attempted assassination at about 25% before November." One wonders whether protesters realize that violence against Trump and his supporters only proves Trump right.

Trump haters might oppose Trump for his anti-democratic ways, but they can't be taken seriously if they too encourage their own anti-democratic ways. They might say that desperate times call for desperate measures—Trump is a bully and can only be stopped by using bullying tactics. Some bystanders will sympathize. And yet the ends can't justify the means. If we lower our standards to defeat an obvious threat to our standards, then we become what we despise. Machiavellianism isn't becoming of Americans, much less those protesting Machiavellianism.

The most democratic way to protest the election of Trump would be to move to another country. Of course, this common threat is counter-productive because many of those who would leave the country to protest are so despised by regular Americans as to encourage them to vote for Trump just to precipitate the mass exodus.

A third-party option would be nice, though none of the talked about candidates offer a Classical Liberal anything to get excited about. Ultimately, the best we might be able to hope for is that this circus-like election cycle proves how distorted our system truly is, and how much reform is necessary. If nothing else, it will agitate reform of the various systems that Trump is exploiting, and that should be positive whether or not he makes it to the White House.

—March 2016

IF YOU THINK THIS IS ABOUT SEXISM AND RACISM, YOU'RE MISSING THE POINT

AT FIRST, IT WAS ENTERTAINING to watch the talking heads try to make sense of the election results that they had been so wrong in predicting.

Then, it got scary.

As the results came in, and it became clear that Donald Trump would win the presidency, it seemed as though a light bulb flashed in their heads: Half of America is sexist and racist. Nothing else could explain this election of such a vile creature to the highest position in the land.

The musician Moby posted a meme that captured the consensus grief: "America, you are so much more racist and misogynistic than I'd ever imagined." People wept in public at the clear evidence that America hates women, Hispanics, African Americans, Muslims, and LBGT types.

It is an understandable frustration considering the kind of rhetoric that Trump has espoused over the last year. The thought is that, since some 60 million Americans voted for a misogynistic, xenophobic bigot, some 60 million Americans must be misogynistic, xenophobic bigots. As an emotional Van Jones put it: "This was a white-lash against a changing country. It was a white-lash against a black president, in part. And that's the part where the pain comes."

But can that really be what's happening?

First of all, if it were simply a racist referendum against a black president, it would have happened in 2012 for Obama's second term. If it were a sexist referendum against a female leader, then why did so many vote for a female vice president in 2008? Why were there so many black, Hispanic, and women votes for Trump?

Ultimately, if it really were the case that half of America was so bigoted, we'd be facing a problem so great that not even the Constitution could save us.

Perhaps there is another explanation.

Revolt of the Masses

The fact is, this election mirrors a pattern that we've seen across the globe in the last several years. We saw it in Brexit; we saw it in the bailout referendum in Greece. What links these is not sex or race, but economic hardship and a general populist rejection of a globalist, anti-traditional modernity that is being force-fed to average people. And, though race and sex play a factor here, it is lazy to simply vilify half of America as bigots and blame them. The issue is deeper and requires a subtler analysis.

The best pre-election explanation of the Trump vote came from Michael Moore, who, despite his crassness, nailed the sentiment of a vast contingent of middle-Americans, who have for several decades now been trampled on and overlooked in favor of an increasingly hostile liberal elite.

As Moore puts it: "Donald Trump came to the Detroit Economic Club and stood there in front of Ford Motor executives and said 'if you close these factories as you're planning to do in Detroit and build them in Mexico, I'm going to put a 35% tariff on those cars when you send them back and nobody's going to buy them.' It was an amazing thing to see. No politician, Republican or Democrat, had ever said anything like that to these executives, and it was music to the ears of people in Michigan and Ohio and Pennsylvania and Wisconsin — the 'Brexit' states."

The revolt is about a group of people who have been disenfranchised by decades of laws that have marginalized them in favor of the formerly marginalized. As pointed out in works like Robert Putnam's *Bowling Alone*, Charles Murray's *Coming Apart*, and J.D. Vance's *Hillbilly Elegy*, since WWII, the United States government has engaged in a systematic dismantling of white middle class America, through taxes, regulations, globalism, multiculturalism, political correctness, and a destruction of fundamental Christian values of marriage and family. And this vote for Trump has been a natural rebellion against that effort.

REMEDIATION OF REMEDIATION

In this light, it is clear that sex and race do play a role in this election, but it isn't so in the way that the Left presents it. That is, it's not an antagonism against women, Hispanics, African Americans, Muslims, and LBGT types, but rather a defense against them. The straight white Christian male has been vilified and dumped on for decades now, and has been persuaded to conform to a world that hates him. For many, it is not antagonism, but rather self-preservation.

Granted, the various penalties and punishments levied upon straight white males has been based in legitimate grievances. The underprivileged and minority groups have been badly treated for centuries. But the reparations have taken the form of similar bad treatment, so-called 'remedial discrimination', thus presenting a second wrong to make right. Moreover, it has been levied against people who had nothing to do with the original bad treatment, creating a sense of great injustice among the new victims of discrimination.

Regard Lena Dunham's blithe request that straight white men become extinct. Evidently, though it has long since been atrocious to suggest such a thing for women and minorities, proposing the wholesale extermination of straight white males is considered progress.

It turns out, if you vilify, castigate, belittle, and dehumanize a people long enough, they will get sick of it and fight back. It is curious that liberal elites could not predict that.

And so now it seems as though straight white males are the underclass, and are the disadvantaged ones who now seek justice. The pendulum of discrimination has swung back the other way. Take, as an example, how one group has thought it necessary to develop a scholarship for underprivileged whites. The mere sound of it is like a foreign language. And yet, if we can get beyond the initial shock of the concept, we see that it actually makes sense. If everyone else has one, why not for whites? They are poor and in need of assistance too. Everyone says discrimination is bad, but they practice it blatantly in effort to support everyone other than white males. It only makes sense that such a group will do what they can to protect and support themselves.

This election (and other similar referendums around the globe) are a statement that this group has had enough of the hatred and conformity, and is now fighting back. It is about sexism and racism inasmuch as this group has been the victim of institutionalized sexism and racism for decades, and are now finally done putting up with it. Some will say that, as evidenced by this election, half of America is sexist and racist. But, if they say that, then we'd have to admit that actually the whole country is sexist and racist because Hillary's plan would have further continued the remedial discrimination that has plagued a population since the '40s.

As David Wong of Cracked put it, "It feels good to dismiss people, to mock them, to write them off as deplorables. But you might as well take time to try to understand them, because I'm telling you, they'll still be around long after Trump is gone."

Pendulum Swings

Moore's video ends abruptly when Moore says voting for Trump and sticking it to the system will feel good. But he doesn't end there. In the full documentary, he goes on to say that it will feel good for a while, but that it will be a short lived euphoria that will be followed by the same issues that led them to voting for Trump in the first place.

In other words, a Trump victory is a band-aid that will leave the real wound festering.

Moore has never been more correct. That is because the policies that Trump will instate might help the straight white male contingent for a while, but will also swing the pendulum back the other way to oppress the others.

And so we will shortly be in another situation that will require more reparation. It will be an endless tug of war that can only leave a lot of people muddy. Soon, Trump supporters will see that he was not the answer, and that the only thing that can truly solve this riddle is if we finally get rid of all discrimination, direct and remedial. Only then can we actually achieve true equality and find peace between our diverse populations.

Perhaps this election will help people realize this. It won't be easy, and Americans of all stripes will need to 'deal with it' for it to work.

May heaven help us.

—November, 2016

TRUMP-
HATING
TOWARD
TOTALI-
TARIANISM

IN THE CLIMAX OF THE classic *Pirates of Silicon Valley*, Steve Jobs is shown presenting his iconic 1984 Big Brother commercial before his adoring audience. IBM is the tyrant and Apple is the revolutionary who takes them down. Everyone cheers. But, as Big Brother's voice thunders over the crowd, Jobs' associate points to Bill Gates backstage. Big Brother isn't IBM—it's Microsoft, the company Apple had just teamed up with to take on IBM. A sinking feeling comes over the idealistic young Jobs. To defeat the enemy, they had become the enemy.

It is a picture of our age. Anyone who reads *The New York Times* knows that Trump was an Orwellian monster who had to be taken down at all costs. And yet, to do so, anti-Trumpers waged a four-year political war in which every brand of intimidation, censorship, incitement, baseless accusation, and character assassination was employed. As everyone gathered in the socially un-distanced streets to celebrate defeating the great orange tyrant, someone somewhere was pointing at the political Left. To slay the monster, they had become the monster.

At a campaign rally in October, Trump said, "If Democrats are willing to cause such destruction in the pursuit of power, just imagine the destruction they would cause if they ever obtained the power they crave." Since the election, we don't have to imagine. We see it unfolding before us.

We need look no further than the eerie list-making of Trump supporters that cropped up in the lead up to and aftermath of the election. It began in early 2020 as commentators pondered what the post-Trump world would be like. In July, *Atlantic* columnist Anne Applebaum warned in a not-so-subtle overture to independent voters that history would judge Trump collaborators and enablers in the same way that history judged Hitler collaborators and enablers.

In October, economic advisor Robert Reich tweeted, "When this nightmare is over, we need a Truth and Reconciliation Commission. It would erase Trump's lies, comfort those who have been harmed by his hatefulness, and name every official, politician, executive, and media mogul whose greed and cowardice enabled this catastrophe." Up sprang the Trump Accountability Project to do just that.

Emboldened by the historic election, speculation turned into a full campaign. Alexandria Ocasio-Cortez joined the chorus: "Is anyone archiving these Trump sycophants for when they try to downplay or deny their complicity in the future? I foresee decent probability of many deleted Tweets, writings, photos in the future." she tweeted Nov. 6. Hollywood types boldly foot-stomped the concept. "Never forget these enablers," Zach Braff tweeted. "#RememberWhoSaidNothing," Chris Evans added.

As election results firmed up and Trump's litigation failed to overturn the outcome, rhetoric creeped toward threats. "A word of warning to those sending money to the Trump legal team at this point. This could later be considered to be a crime making you an accessory, if this stunt is deemed to be a coup attempt under President Biden," Adam Schiff tweeted. A striking claim coming from a congressman who spent the previous four years trying to unseat the duly elected president of the United States.

Now, these musings can be spun in a number of ways. AOC can make anything seem unthreatening by adding an 'lol'. But the fascistic undercurrent cannot be denied: These leftists mean to identify and punish political enemies once they are back in power. It doesn't take a PhD in Political Science to know that this is at the core of fascism.

An unhinged Keith Olbermann gave the game away: "Trump can be and must be expunged. The hate he has triggered, the Pandora's box he has opened, they will not be so easily destroyed. So, let us brace ourselves. The task is twofold. The terrorist Trump must be defeated, must be destroyed, must be devoured at the ballot box and then he and his enablers and his supporters and his collaborators and the Mike Lees and the William Barrs and the Sean Hannitys and the Mike Pences and the Rudy Giulianis and the Kyle Rittenhouses and the Amy Coney Barretts must be prosecuted and convicted and removed from our society while we try and rebuild it."

Anyone who watches the Olbermann clip will be struck by his fervor. His rabid, snarling speech isn't reminiscent of a journalist conveying a story or even an activist hoping to make a practical solution to a shared problem, but of a militant totalitarian with a one-track mind. He fancies himself a modern Edward R. Murrow, but his thrust is more like that of Paul J. Goebbels.

THE TOTALITARIAN MIND

The wide-eyed observer will wonder how it came to this. How could anyone who considers himself a lower-case 'd' democrat insinuate the most capital 'T' Totalitarian things? How could people who decry fascism actually participate in the very ethos that they are supposedly fighting?

An easy explanation is to point to Trump. Leftist firebrands like Olbermann and AOC assume that, since Trump is so terrible, they have license to be just as terrible. Like toddlers, they yell, "He started it!" and all is justified. If your goal is to take down the monster, it's okay to become your own monster.

But any reader of history knows that this is exactly how totalitarianism comes about. Totalitarians don't suddenly appear out of the blue and start tyrannizing the people. The people must ask for it. And what makes them ask for tyranny? It starts with a profound hatred for a group or people. As Hannah Arendt explained in *The Origins of Totalitarianism*, the Soviet and Nazi regimes were only possible because the average citizens had been primed to the totalitarian mind. Arendt explains that a people must pass through three stages before they arrive at the totalitarianism that we know: The first is what we might call 'Bugbearism', where a people derives its self-identity from the hatred of another people or group; the second is 'Existentialism', where conflict with the bugbear is seen as a threat to the people's existence; and the third is 'Purificationism', where the people resolves to eradicate the problem by any means. A brief reflection of each reveals just how closely our current path follows the pattern:

STAGE I: BUGBEARISM

Around the time of the 2016 election a meme surfaced comparing the rise of Trump to the rise of Hitler. The argument was that the terror didn't start with concentration camps and gas chambers; it started with divisive rhetoric and otherism. Totalitarians need to rally their people. And the best way to rally their people is against another people. While despots had always propped up foreign peoples as the foe, the totalitarian innovation was to identify a faction of the domestic people as the hated group.

Every totalitarian regime has its bugbear. For the Nazis it was the Communists and Jews. For the Soviets it was the Kulaks. For Maoists it was intellectuals. In each case, the bugbear was painted in such a terrible light as to elicit fear and loathing in the most innocent of citizens.

Since the hated group is integrated into the society, a campaign must be made to distinguish them. Disagreements are proven to be based on inherent differences and differences are so irreconcilable that 'they' seem to be another species. This is why talk turns so swiftly to dehumanizing. These others are not really humans—they are vermin, termites, pestilence. When the enemy is not human, it is much easier to hate them.

Of course, Trump had his bugbears, namely illegal immigrants and Islamic fundamentalists—foreign threats that every U.S. president since Clinton had battled. Trump's campaign promises of building a border wall and prohibiting travel from Muslim countries drew criticism from modern and classical liberals alike, and cemented his critics' perception of him as racist and xenophobic.

Today's leftists have a bugbear too—Trump and his followers. Since this bugbear is domestic, the Left must do a job of distinguishing them. By the reports of Facebook commentators and mainstream media, these people are not only uneducated and bigoted, but outright sociopathic war criminals. Indeed, they are so vile as to be seen as less than human. Olbermann referred to them as "maggots", a term which has a distinguished history in totalitarian rhetoric. Tune into a leftist social media echo chamber and you'll see just how pervasive this dehumanizing is.

Real Bugbearism occurs when a people self-identifies with their hatred of the enemy. Arendt said that "Nazi propaganda was ingenious enough to transform antisemitism into a principle of self-definition, and thus to eliminate it from the fluctuations of mere opinion." It is the difference between community and tribalism as David Brooks puts it: "Community is mutual love of a thing. Tribalism is mutual hate of another." And who can deny that this is happening throughout America? It might be said that Trump's rise and popularity have come about, not because of any of his merits but rather because he stands as a fearless counter to the Left. The anti-Trump movement's label speaks for itself.

Stage II: Existentialism

In a recent study, researchers found that totalitarian tendencies are more likely to arise in societies where there is a high prevalence of deadly diseases. The explanation is simple: People are willing to do away with freedoms in order to protect themselves from an existential threat. The free movement of individuals and assembly of groups is how pathogens spread, and so there is an instinct to put up borders, increase rules, and limit freedom to stop that spread.

Tyrants exploit this phenomenon in a couple of ways. First, they emphasize the risks of any pathogens that might be present. Note that one of Hitler's first initiatives was to fumigate the factories to clear out tuberculosis. They can also manipulate this tendency simply by making any situation into a life-and-death matter. If people believe their lives are at risk, they will react as if they were. Existentialism leads to fear and fear opens the door for control. As Camus put it, "The welfare of humanity is always the alibi of tyrants."

The Left has embraced this strategy wholesale. Old school liberal Mark Lila explained how today's leftists are heirs of the 1960s civil rights movement, which was successful primarily because it was made into a moral issue by religious leaders such as Martin Luther King. Based on the success of that movement, leftists learned that they can gain an upper hand in an argument just by moralizing it and turning anyone who disagrees into a moral monster. The way that they do this is by making everything into a matter of life-and-death, even when there is no clear danger.

These days, every matter is of the gravest moral concern: Systemic racism is tantamount to genocide, transphobia is killing people; climate change will bring about the end of the world. Anyone who watched the 2020 DNC will recognize the refrain: 'Vote like your life depends on it, because it does.' And how often does one hear the statement 'People are dying!' as if to settle the case?

Of course, there is the Coronavirus Pandemic, which started as an actual disease but has since become strictly moral since. The message is unequivocal: If you do not wear a mask or if you gather with other people, then you are responsible for the deaths of more than 300,000 Americans. Indeed, since it is assumed that the science is so clear and the experts have warned us of the dangers, you are not only responsible for the deaths, it is assumed that you actually want all the people to die. Trump was not simply being optimistic when he tried to downplay the risks, he was being a devious tyrant out to kill as many Americans as he could. 'He has blood on his hands', as critics will say.

We see this across the board. If one disagrees with the radical Marxist agenda of Black Lives Matter, he is racist supporting the genocide of African Americans. If a man supports traditional gender roles, he is pushing toxic masculinity and rape culture. If a teacher doesn't think children should be placed on puberty blockers, he is contributing to the bullying and abuse of millions of children. If you disagree, it cannot be because you have a well-founded argument or even a diverse perspective, but rather because you have some sort of phobia or sociopathy.

The goal is to gain an upper hand in debates. But, as Lila warned, the effect is to undermine efforts that are actually moral. If everything's an existential crisis, nothing is. At the same time, it ultimately removes the possibility for debate. If a person is not allowed to disagree without being labeled a sociopath, there is no civil recourse. They either agree or must be eliminated from society, a condition that cannot end well.

STAGE III: PURIFICATIONISM

Once the bugbear is painted as a moral monster, anything is justified to oust them. Not only are transgressions excused to do so; they are encouraged. As a matter of social justice, they aren't even necessary evils, they are necessary goods—duties—to rid us of the existential threat.

One of the earliest figures to voice this mentality was a Russian Maximalist named Ivan Pavlov (no relation to the Nobel-winning psychologist of the same name). This earlier Pavlov wrote a tract entitled 'The Purification of Mankind', in which he divided the people into two 'races': 'exploiters' and 'exploited'. Pavlov concluded that the exploiter race was "morally inferior to our animal predecessors," and had to be exterminated by the morally superior race of the exploited class. In one prescient essay, Pavlov demonstrated all three stages in the totalitarian mind, from identifying the bugbear to presenting them as an existential threat to the solution of exterminating them.

Wholesale murder is not the only method of purification. Perhaps it is worse what totalitarians do with the truth. Totalitarians also employ social isolation, silencing, censorship, blacklisting, and psychological manipulation such as gaslighting to remove the trouble group from society. Orwell spoke of 'unpersoning', the Stalinist way of removing from pictures and history anyone who had become politically inconvenient. Anything to purify our land of the blight that is threatening us.

Any dispassionate participant will recognize that this is exactly what is going on today. Though the political Left has not quite made it to concentration camps and extermination yet, they have made unpersoning into an art. Thanks to an overwhelming coalition of mainstream media, academia, big tech, and governmental bodies, the Left has been able to monopolize political discourse, dispel contradictory perspectives, and ostracize anyone who disagrees. To chronicle a few of the more striking examples from this year:

In June, in response to the BLM protests at the time, conservative commentator Heather McDonald wrote a piece bringing into question the narrative of police racism. She cited a scientific study published in a respected peer-reviewed journal as her central evidence. But as soon as the study's authors realized their work had been used to undermine the argument for systemic racism, they disavowed their study and the journal retracted it. It was not taken down because it lacked scientific rigor or presented false conclusions, but because the authors believed the information was being used in a dangerous way.

Around the same time, as George Floyd protests erupted across American cities, a group of self-described health professionals, students, and activists published an open letter stating that the protests didn't pose a COVID risk because they were fighting the public health risk of racism.

And then there was the Stalin-esque 'disappearing' of Hunter Biden's laptop. First, the paper that broke the story *The New York Post* was muzzled over anti-piracy rules. Then, when it had become clear that it wasn't piracy, mainstream media called it Russian disinformation and ignored the story. Only after the election did some outlets finally begin to cover the bombshell.

These, coupled with countless other examples, as well as the constant campaign to demonetize, shadow-ban, and cancel anyone who does not conform to the leftist narrative amount to the greatest propaganda campaign since the lead-up to the Second World War. No one dedicated to liberal democracy can justify the brazen censorship and gaslighting that legacy media outlets and social media companies have engaged in during the last year.

Ultimately, concentration camps and extermination are not wholly unthinkable in this climate. With AOC's list-making and Olbermann's bombast, and a relentless assault by the media, even normal people have begun to think that violence is acceptable. I recall several seemingly mild-mannered young professional women celebrating the death and destruction inflicted during the George Floyd riots. When questioned, their justification was that the violence was necessary because the message wouldn't have been heard otherwise.

Meanwhile, more militant factions are not even hiding their motives. The man who attempted to assassinate GOP senators at a baseball practice in 2017 was a member of groups called 'Terminate the Republicans' and 'The Road to Hell Is Paved with Republicans'. The man who killed a Trump supporter during a Portland rally said he was "100% ATIFA" and "ready for war". Evidently, ideas have consequences.

TRUMP-HATING TOWARD TOTALITARIANISM

In July, a group of prominent liberals in media and academia including J. K. Rowling, Cornel West, and Noam Chomsky voiced their concerns over the cancel culture storm which has been raging the last five years or so. In the letter, they acknowledged that Trump is a threat to democracy but suggested that resistance could lead to a dogmatic coercion that would be just as bad or worse. It was a levelheaded and well-articulated plea for free thought and free expression. The fact that hardcore leftists then disparaged and tried to cancel the signers of the letter proves how fargone the Left has become.

As former *New York Times* Editor Bari Weiss said, we need to "stop being shocked" at the totalitarian tendencies of the Left. The forces driving the political Left at this moment are hostile to critical thinking, free expression, and liberal democracy in general, and can only lead to totalitarianism. If you listen to the most honest commentators of the movement, you'll realize that is their clear end and hating Trump was just the means.

—December 2020

HOW TO
AVOID CIVIL
WAR

IF THERE'S ONE THING EVERYONE agrees upon in the lead up to the election, it's that we all disagree.

We disagree on pretty much every major issue: abortion, climate, police, welfare, healthcare, you name it. To some, the American people disagree so much that the inevitable result will be a second civil war.

But if the American system breaks down and we see martial conflict between the Left and the Right, it won't be because we disagree. It will be because we can't agree to disagree. It is the ability to agree to disagree that has long been America's saving grace. And it is our condition without that key buffer that makes talk of civil war so much more common—and realistic.

To begin, it must be admitted that disagreement is nothing new. A quick glance at history shows that we have always had fierce disagreement in this country. Witness Jefferson and Adams in 1796 and 1800, the 1860 election that spurred the first civil war, of course, and the 1876 election that prompted the Compromise of 1877. One might almost think that bitter conflict is a part of the nation's fabric.

Disagreement only becomes a crisis when one person's way of doing something is imposed upon everyone else. And that is exactly the condition we find ourselves in. To an increasing degree, our highly-regulated, interdependent welfare state forces conformity. The more we are taxed, the more we are interested in what's going on in Washington. The more laws we are forced to comply with, the more determined we will be to ensure those laws meet our standards.

To quote one of the great films of all time: "There's two kinds of dumb—a guy that gets naked and runs out in the snow and barks at the moon, and a guy who does the same thing in my living room. First one don't matter. The second one you're kinda forced to deal with." We aren't in a crisis these days because others are naked and barking at the moon. We're in a crisis because they're doing it in our living room.

The presidential election offers the clearest example. The candidate one votes for has long been a source of disagreement and even conflict. But these days it seems it is a matter of life and death. If you listen to the TV personalities and politicians, a victory for the other side would mean the end of the American way of life—in fact, it would actually mean people would die. This is exactly how the Democrats and Republicans have framed the 2020 election. Michelle Obama said that we have to vote "like our lives depend on it". Trump Jr. said that the election was shaping up to be "church, work, and school versus rioting, looting, and vandalism".

A friend recently posted a seemingly benign statement that "politics isn't life". The responses were almost entirely to the contrary. "It's easy for white males to be ambivalent, but people of color depend on politics to survive", they argued. In the modern welfare state, they have a point: These days, politics *is* life. And that is why the election has become so important.

DEMOCRATIC TOTALITARIANISM.

The reason it's so hard to agree to disagree is based on the size and scope of government. The larger the state is and the more aspects of our lives it affects, the more interconnected we become, and the less we are able to differ. A vote for president or even congress affects a large portion of each of our lives. And so, if the opposition gets elected, a large portion of our lives will be negatively affected.

The classical liberal model is sensible: Everything not forbidden is allowed. But we have become victim of the totalitarian bias: Everything not forbidden is compulsory. It can only bring struggle, competition for power, and life-and-death elections.

The next step is obvious, though few utter it. That is because, when an election is a matter of life and death, then people will be willing to die to ensure it goes their way. That means exasperated pleas on social media. That means intimidation on the streets. That means armed conflict at the voting booths.

Those who have grown alarmed by the discord in America will seek ways to de-escalate. Naturally, many will think that can only happen when we find common ground and come to some agreement. And, while I admire those who endeavor to unite the disparate sides of the debate, I don't think it's plausible and it might not even be necessary.

Rather, to avoid civil war, we ought to figure out ways, not to agree, but to agree to disagree. The less interdependent we are, the more we will be able to live in peace with diverse people and groups.

—October 2020